Highlights of Ep

Technical editing: J&M

On the cover: Gate of Mazaeus and Mithridates in Ephesus

ISBN: 978-83-66950-02-3 (paperback)
ISBN: 978-83-66950-03-0 (ePub)

Publisher: Aslan Publishing House

Contact: contact@turkisharchaeonews.net
Facebook: https://www.facebook.com/turkisharchaeonews
WWW: https://turkisharchaeonews.net/

First Edition. March 2024.

Izabela Miszczak

Highlights of Ephesus

Contents

Preface

Situated in the Aegean region of Turkey, Ephesus is probably one of the best-preserved ancient cities in the Mediterranean. In ancient times, both in the Greek and in the Roman periods, it was a bustling trading city and a centre of worship of Artemis, the Greek goddess of the hunt and the wilderness, but also childbirth and chastity. Later, it became a thriving Christian city with the first of the churches dedicated to Mary, the mother of Christ.

In order to imagine what life was like in the ancient city of the Roman Empire, walk the streets of Ephesus, visit public toilets and residential houses, and then sit back in the great theatre or have a look at the splendid library. Ephesus offers all these things, and many more, to curious travellers who want to be sure that they can make the most of their visit there.

This book offers a guided tour of the most important sights in Ephesus, the absolutely must-see ones. It was created with the thought of the visitors who have limited time on their hands and want to be sure that they will not miss any highlights of the famous ancient city. There are 18 chapters devoted to particular locations within Ephesus, and they are organised geographically.

Thus, we start the tour at the region near the Lower Gate, in the northern part of the site, and finish at the Upper Gate near the State Agora. Each chapter provides a detailed description of the location and its history, as well as its exact location with a GPS coordinates and a QR code to scan that will lead you to the exact spot. Also, every chapter has a photograph of the described location. Finally, the general plan shows the whole site of Ephesus with the relevant locations clearly marked, while the detailed plan magnifies the area of the Curetes Street where the majority of the described objects are situated.

Introduction

Brief history

According to the Greek tradition, Ephesus was founded by a prince called Androklos, the legitimate son of Codrus the king of Athens, who intended to settle in Asia Minor. Before setting off, he had consulted the oracle. As an answer, he heard the enigmatic advice to choose the place indicated by a fish and a wild boar. Oracles were renowned for their unclear statements, but this did not discourage the prince, as he started the search for the perfect spot. One day, while he was preparing a meal of roasted fish, one of them jumped out of the fire, while a lump of burning coal fell into the bushes and scared away a wild boar. It was a clear sign for Androklos that indicated the right place for a new settlement.

However, the area of Ephesus was inhabited from the times much earlier than the arrival of the Greek settlers. As a result of archaeological excavations carried out on the nearby mounds called Arvalya and Çukuriçi, it was proved that the human settlement in the area dates back to the 7th millennium BCE, i.e. the Neolithic period.

Before the Greeks arrived at the area where later the famous Artemision was erected, there had stood a sanctuary dedicated to the mother goddess Cybele, venerated by local people. Later, Cybele was identified by the Greeks with the goddess Artemis of the Olympic pantheon. Many of the features of Cybele were also assigned to Artemis, who became the most important goddess on the Ionian coast of the Aegean Sea. Ephesus was known as an important place of worship of Artemis.

The recent archaeological discoveries within Ephesus revealed the existence of Iron Age Greek pottery dating back to the 11th century BCE. Since its numbers outweigh the handmade indigenous wares, it is assumed that Ephesus was a Greek settlement from the late 11th century BCE. These profound changes in the material culture indicate the early arrival of the Greeks during the Ionian Colonization.

Initially, Ephesus was ruled by kings, and then — by an oligarchy of magnates. In the first half of the 7th century BCE, the city was conquered and destroyed by the nomadic tribe of Cimmerians that terrorised Anatolia, looting Phrygia and Lydia. The Cimmerians destroyed, among others, the first shrine of Artemis of the Ephesians.

Ephesus was rebuilt and again gained importance in the second half of the 7th century BCE when it was controlled by tyrants. After a popular revolt, the city was ruled by a council and entered the golden age of its existence, becoming home to many eminent personalities. Certainly, the most famous inhabitant of Ephesus in this era was the Pre-Socratic philosopher Heraclitus. He used to express his views in a vague and allegorical manner. He is known primarily as the author of the phrases: "No man ever steps in the same river twice" and "Panta rhei" — "Everything flows".

The Temple of Artemis at Ephesus was a great building belonging to the Seven Wonders of the Ancient World. Also known as the Artemision, it certainly deserved the reputation as one of the wonders of the world. It was the largest building in the Hellenistic world, surpassing even the Athenian Parthenon, and was also the first monumental structure built entirely of marble. Unfortunately, nowadays, a visit to the Artemision of Ephesus brings a huge disappointment because only a single re-erected column and a bit of rubble have remained from this once magnificent building to our times.

Ephesus is also an important place for the Christians. Here was one of the first Christian communities in Asia Minor, and Saint John held the position of the Bishop of Ephesus. He mentioned the city in the Book of Revelation, where the city was listed as one of the Seven Churches of Asia Minor, along with Smyrna, Pergamum, Thyatira, Sardis, Philadelphia, and Laodicea.

Saint John spent the last years of his life in Ephesus. He died around 100 CE and was buried on Ayasoluk Hill. Initially, there was a commemorative plaque on his grave. In the 4th century CE, it was encased in a chapel with a wooden roof. In the 6th century CE, the Byzantine Emperor Justinian ordered the construction of a huge basilica on this site. The Church of the Holy Apostles in Constantinople served as the model for its architects.

The construction of the temple was completed in 565. The builders used the elements from the conveniently located nearby Temple of Artemis. The Basilica of Saint John soon became an important destination for pilgrims from all over the Christian world. It was believed that the dust from the tomb of the Apostle possessed healing properties.

After the invasion of the Arabs in the years 654-655, Ephesus fell into decline. The urban life began to focus around Ayasoluk Hill, in a place now known as Selçuk. To prevent damage to the basilica by the Arab raids, a hilltop castle was built, and the temple was surrounded by thick walls. The fortified gate, made of stones obtained from Roman buildings, including the stadium, has been preserved to modern times.

Archaeological research

The history of archaeological research in Ephesus dates back to 1863 when British engineer John Turtle Wood began searching for the remains of the Temple of Artemis. Six years later, he succeeded in identifying its location and then dedicated five years to the excavations in this area.

The next round of archaeological works in Ephesus took place from 1895 to 1913 and was conducted by German and Austrian archaeologists under the direction of Otto Benndorf and Carl Humann. In 1898, Benndorf founded the Austrian Archaeological Institute, which has been conducting archaeological studies in Ephesus for over a century now.

The artefacts found in Ephesus are scattered over many museums around the world. The nearest one is the Ephesus Museum in Selçuk, but there are also many interesting exhibits in the Archaeological Museum and the Museum of History and Art in Izmir. The British Museum in London holds the earliest finds from Ephesus while the Ephesos Museum in Vienna has many of the most spectacular finds from the second phase of the excavations in the early 1900s.

VISITOR TIPS

The Ephesus archaeological site is open to visitors daily. The regular entrance ticket to Ephesus does not include the entry to the Terrace Houses, but this additional expense is definitely worth its price.

There are two gates to the archaeological site of Ephesus. The Upper Gate is situated in the south-eastern part of the site, near the ancient Magnesia Gate. The Lower Gate is in the northern part of the archaeological site, near the theatre. This guidebook follows the route from the Lower Gate to the Upper Gate and all the stops of the tour are described in this order.

Most of the organised groups of tourists choose the Upper Gate as the starting point because the walk is downhill in this direction. Thus, if you visit early in the morning, select the Lower Gate to see the theatre and the Celsus Library before the crowds get there from the Upper Gate. The evening visit is best started from the Upper Entrance as the organised tours are long gone. There are car parks, souvenir stalls, toilets, and taxi stands at both entrances.

Before setting out for the tour, remember to take bottled water and appropriate protection from the sun, as it is difficult to find shaded areas on the site and there are no shops, bars, or vending machines there. Smoking is strictly forbidden in all the areas of Ephesus. Because of ongoing archaeological and restoration works, some buildings or sections of the ancient city may be temporarily unavailable for visitors.

At the Upper Gate, near the State Agora, there is a 3D model of ancient Ephesus, with its most characteristic buildings reconstructed. It is worthwhile to spend a couple of minutes there, in order to understand the spatial arrangement of the city, squeezed in between two hills and connected to the harbour. However, to see a much more detailed model, it is necessary to visit the Ephesos Museum in Vienna.

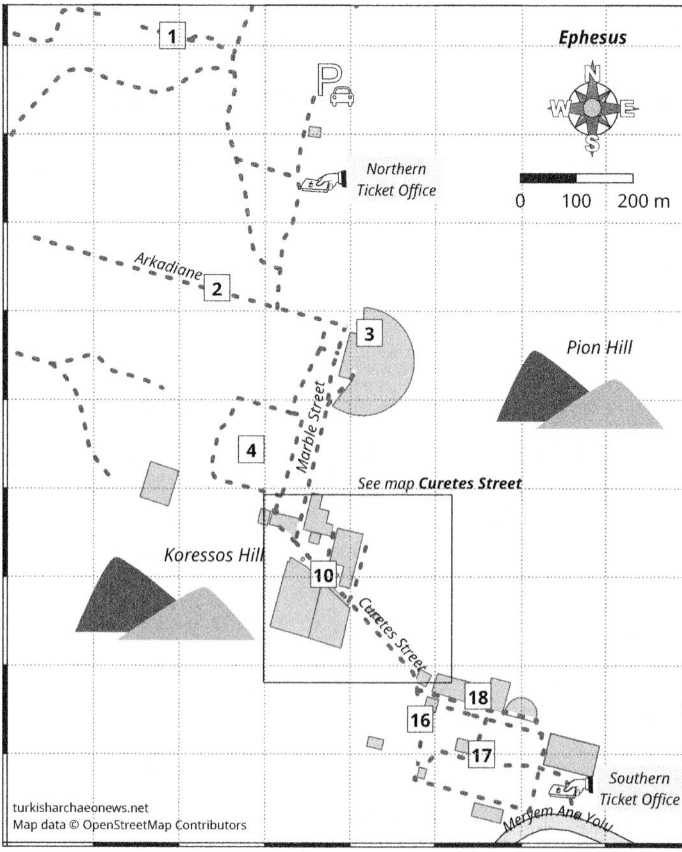

1 Church of the Virgin Mary
2 Arcadiane Street
3 Great Theatre
4 Commercial Agora
10 Curetes Street
16 Domitian Square and the Temple of the Imperial Cult
17 State Agora
18 Public buildings to the north of the State Agora

Note: each object is described in a separate chapter

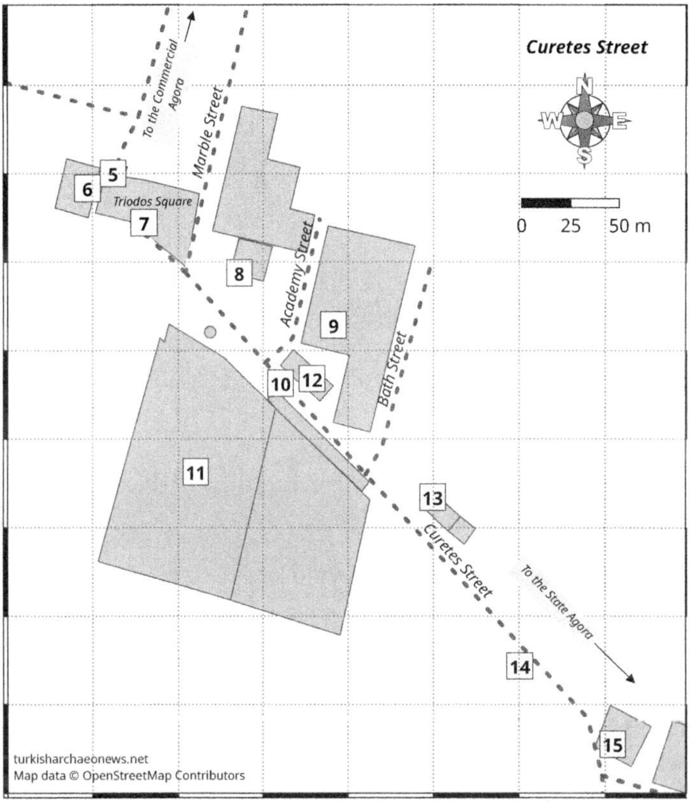

5 Gate of Mazaeus and Mithridates
6 Library of Celsus
7 Triodos Square
8 Public latrines
9 Scholastica Baths
10 Curetes Street
11 Terrace Houses
12 Temple of Hadrian
13 Trajan's Nymphaeum
14 Alytarches' Stoa
15 Hydreion and Memmius Monument

Note: each object is described in a separate chapter

Church of the Virgin Mary

GPS coordinates: 37.944983, 27.339413

The Church of the Virgin Mary was the first of churches dedicated to the mother of Christ. It is also the most significant building from Christian times in Ephesus. It was erected in the 3rd century within an earlier building. Architecturally, the structure can be described as a basilica with a nave and two aisles. The aisles were divided into shorter parts, which could serve as shops. Today, the best-preserved section of the structure is a cylindrical baptistery, located in the northern part of the atrium.

St. Mary at Ephesus - fact or myth?

It is worth remembering that Mary, the mother of Christ, was not the first woman honoured in Ephesus. The city had a long tradition of religious worship of female deities. The first of them had been a local Anatolian goddess Cybele who was later merged with the Greek goddess Artemis. The huge temple erected to the latter – the Artemision of Ephesus – was once considered one of the Seven Wonders of the World.

The Artemision, 115 meters long and 55 meters wide, covered the area 1.5 times larger than the Church of Mary. The Artemision also had much more elegant proportions because the Church of Mary had an unusually elongated plan, resulting from its construction inside an earlier building.

There was an exceptional reason why the church in Ephesus was dedicated to Mary. According to the local tradition, the mother of Christ arrived at Ephesus together with St. John and spent the

Church of the Virgin Mary

last years of her life there. Although there is no decisive historical evidence to support this belief, there are some premises supporting it. The most significant one is the presence of St. John in Ephesus, who started writing his gospel there. He was also buried in this city, and the basilica was erected in his name.

Jesus, before dying on the cross, as it is explained in the Gospel of John, entrusted St. John to take care of Jesus' mother, Mary. John the Evangelist stated that Jesus, during the crucifixion, declared the adoption of him as the son of Mary: "Near the cross of Jesus stood his mother, his mother's sister, Mary the wife of Clopas, and Mary Magdalene. When Jesus saw his mother there, and the disciple whom he loved standing nearby, he said to her, 'Woman, here is your son,' and to the disciple, 'Here is your mother.' From that time on, this disciple took her into his home."

According to a tradition recorded by Irenaeus and Eusebius of Caesarea, John later came to Ephesus where he worked and finally died; it is assumed that he brought with him his adopted mother. These faint hints provided the basis for the early belief that Mary also lived in Ephesus with John. However, the evidence that St. Mary actually stayed there is not forceful, and there are much better indications that her permanent house was in Jerusalem. Nevertheless, the tradition that St. Mary resided and died in Ephesus has been alive until the present times.

The evolution of the Church of St. Mary

In the 3rd century CE, the times of economic crisis began in Ephesus. During this period, the local Christian community built its first church. However, its builders used an older structure clearly related to the pagan cults of the city's past. The spacious area to the north had been occupied by the Olympieion, erected around 130 CE for the Imperial Cult of Emperor Hadrian as Zeus Olympios.

The porticoes surrounded the temple sanctuary, and the Church of Mary was inserted into the southern one. This fact explains the unusual dimensions of the building – it was 145 meters long but only 30 meters wide. An atrium on the square plan and a narthex paved with mosaics led into the church. In later times, two more churches were built inside the ancient building, arranged one behind the other.

One of the most significant events in the history of Ephesus – the third ecumenical council also known as the Council of Ephesus – was convened in 431 by Emperor Theodosius the Younger in the great church of St. Mary. The delegates arrived from as far as Rome, Alexandria, and Antioch, and their number reached 250. The purpose of this council was to settle the dispute caused by Nestorius, the Patriarch of Constantinople, on the understanding of the person of Jesus. Among other issues discussed, there was a disagreement concerning the title of Mary as the Mother of God or the Mother of Christ. The council opted for the first version, establishing an extraordinary theological relationship between Mary and Christ. Thus, from that moment, Mary has always been strongly linked to Ephesus through the decision of the council.

However, later the seat of the bishop was transferred from the Church of St. Mary to St. John's Basilica, possibly in the 7th century. Then, the Church of Mary functioned later as a cemetery church only. It was rebuilt several times, so the structure we can see today does not reflect the appearance of the church from the time of the Council of Ephesus or the later 8th-century building. Instead, it represents the late Byzantine period, when the domed church fell into ruin and was eventually abandoned.

It was replaced by the new basilica, of much smaller dimensions, built into the space of the old church. The new church had the entrance through the apse of the old one, where the opening was cut. This new structure did not have colonnades but walled-up arcades. It was constructed with reused material of various kinds.

The small new church was reconstructed with two additional rows of columns supporting the roof, and the building gained the shape of a five-ailed basilica. Finally, the whole structure collapsed and was turned into a cemetery. It is not known when the collapse happened, but there are mentions of the 'old church' with the icon of the Virgin Mary from the 12th century, so it must have survived at least until this period.

When visiting the ruins today, one may feel some confusion resulting from these multiple phases of rebuilding and transformation. For instance, the old baptistery was used as a profane space where ovens were installed. Moreover, the diaconicon (a chamber where the vestments, books, etc., that are used in the Divine Services of the church are held) of the old church was transformed into the baptistery for the new one. In the northern colonnade of the atrium, a small bath was erected, with several rooms and a hypocaust system. In fact, the significant part of the great church may have been transformed into a residential district while a graveyard surrounded the church.

Today, the best-preserved part of the structure is a cylindrical baptistery, located in the northern part of the atrium. In the central part of the baptistery, there was a pool, where the baptised people could be fully immersed in water.

Buildings near the church

The building to the east of the Church of St. Mary was possibly the seat of the bishop, i.e. episkopeion, but currently the archaeologists prefer to call it simply the Byzantine Palace. This spacious residence is distinguished by the complex architecture and the size, as its total area was astonishingly huge, encompassing 3750 square meters. It consisted of a large bath complex of several rooms and a latrine to the north, a colonnaded courtyard measuring 14 to 8.5 meters, and a prestigious southern wing with grand reception rooms and audience chambers. On the southern side, a chapel was later added to the complex and in time, a cemetery developed around it.

One possible explanation of the function of this complex is that it functioned as a palace of a bishop because of the location very close to the Church of St. Mary. A most peculiar history is related to this residence because it was remodelled under very suspicious circumstances. According to the local legend, the resident of the palace, Bishop Antonius, redecorated his dining room with the columns taken from the Church of Mary and his bath was equipped with marbles from the baptistery. The outrage he had created resulted in his deposition from the office in the year 400.

Alternatively, due to the lavish decorations and the presence of many reception chambers, the palace may have been the residence of the Proconsul of the Province of Asia and, at the later times, the strategos of the Thracesian theme. This version seems to be partially confirmed by the archaeological finds, such as numerous seals from the 8th and the 9th centuries, testifying to the administrative function of the building. However, the villa located above the theatre is the alternative location of the governor's offices.

The palace was abandoned and systematically demolished in the 10th century, and a lime kiln was set up directly at its southern entrance. Sadly, currently almost nothing was visible of the Bishop's Palace, with only the aerial photographs displayed on-site to offer any idea about its appearance. The ruins, excavated in the 20th century, are now completely overgrown with bushes.

To the south of the church, there is a large building identified as the early Byzantine residence, from the early 5th century CE. This spacious residence, described as an urban peristyle villa, covers an impressive area of 1600 square meters, and it has been excavated very recently. The archaeologists discovered that this building was renovated numerous times and its functions varied. In the 6/7th century, the workshops, such as stoves, an oil press, and hand mills, were added to a prestigious wing. Simultaneously, an open courtyard was added to the south of the villa, most probably to function as a grazing ground or a vegetable garden. The close connection between living quarters, handicraft spaces, and agricultural activities was apparent in this period.

While the building itself was damaged in an earthquake that occurred in the 6th century, as testified by deformed floors, it continued to be occupied in the first half of the 7th century. The complex was destroyed, most probably, in the second half of the 7th century, as evidenced by the find of more than 3,500 coins.

Arcadiane Street

GPS coordinates: 37.941956, 27.340110

Arcadiane (Harbour) Street is a colonnaded road, named after Emperor Arcadius, who reigned between 395 and 408 CE. However, this name is misleading because there is strong evidence for the existence of this street in the much earlier Hellenistic period, at least from the 1st century BCE. This theory is supported by exposed fragments and foundations of the Harbour Gate, located on the axis of the road at its western end. Arcadius only rebuilt the earlier road after a series of earthquakes, raising its level.

The street

The street is well-preserved and extends for a distance of more than 500 meters, keeping the width of 11 meters. It starts at the theatre and ends near the ancient harbour. At both ends of the Arcadiane, there were monumental gates in the form of triumphal arches, with three passageways each. However, the gate near to the theatre was destroyed. One can only imagine numerous emperors and ancient celebrities arriving by sea to Ephesus and then walking to the city centre along this ceremonial road.

Arcadiane Street was designed to be the showcase of Ephesus for the newly arrived guests. Interestingly, it was aimed to draw the focus of these visitors to itself and not to the surroundings. The continuous back walls of the side halls completely blocked out the external vistas and isolated the space of the street from the natural environment.

Two walkways for pedestrians, located on both sides of the road,

Arcadiane Street, leading in the direction of the harbour

have a width of 5 meters each. In the past, these Corinthian order porticoes were entirely paved with mosaics. Behind these arcades, there were numerous shops, so walkers could make purchases while strolling along the shaded and sheltered paths, at the same time enjoying the breeze blowing from the sea. Sewage channels ran beneath the marble flagstones of the street.

It is also known from the excavated inscriptions that the road even had street lighting, as stated by Ammianus Marcellinus: "the brilliancy of the lamps [of Arcadiane] at night often equalled the light of day". An inscription discovered during the excavations of the street confirms this claim, as it informs that fifty lamps illuminated the Harbour Street at night. This was a quite rare luxury in the Roman, testifying to the wealth of Ephesus.

In the middle of the road, there were four columns in the Corinthian order, which once held, most probably, the statues of the Four Evangelists. Today, only one of these columns is still standing, while of the other three only the bases have been preserved. These bases have the niches displaying Christian symbols. The columns were erected during the reign of Emperor Justinian in the 6th century CE, as an essential message to the guests of Ephesus, informing them that they were entering a Christian city. However, in the Byzantine period, the street was situated outside the city walls and the erection of these four columns in the 6th century marks the zenith of its last golden age.

Harbour district

The Arcadiane Street led to the harbour district of Ephesus. The harbour quarter of Ephesus is located to the south of the Church of Mary. In ancient times, not one but three gates marked the transfer from sea to land in Ephesus. The Middle Harbor Gate was the earliest one, as it dates back to the reign of Emperor Hadrian. It stood at the western end of the Arcadiane and had three passageways separated by supports, consisting of four Ionic columns. The quality of the gate's architectural decor is outstanding. The Ionic capitals imitate Classical models from the 5th century BCE. Sadly, to see the remaining fragments of the Middle Harbor Gate, one has to visit the Ephesos Museum in Vienna, Austria.

The harbour of Ephesus itself silted up a long time ago and is now a small lake, although there are some ongoing activities by the Turkish authorities to make it functional again. The revitalisation of the harbour means that it will be possible to sail into the ancient city once again.

The main square of the harbour district of Ephesus was the so-called Hall of Verulanus. This spacious square, measuring 200 by 240 meters, used to be the largest of the sports facilities situated along thee Arcadiane Street. Its name comes from the founder, Verulanus, who was the chief priest of Asia during the reign of Emperor Hadrian. He ordered the paving and tiling of the greater of the palestrae of the Harbour Baths with marble slabs in 13 different shades. These panels have not been preserved to our times, but their existence is evidenced by the holes in the walls, where the panels were attached.

This arcaded courtyard served as training grounds for the athletes. Called xystos in antiquity, the court was surrounded by a three-aisled colonnade, with its broad middle aisle serving as a running track. The best opportunity to glimpse the ruined Hall of Verulanus is to look at its eastern corner, recently uncovered by the archaeologists next to the Church of Mary.

Harbour Baths

The ruined Harbour Baths stand to the west of the Hall of Verulanus. However, only a small part of the complex has been excavated so far. Still, the visible remains of the largest architectural complex in the city of Ephesus make a big impression on the visitors. The construction of the Harbour Baths began, most probably, during the reign of Emperor Domitian (81-96 CE). It means that this baths complex is the oldest one that can be seen in Ephesus today, as the other ones were erected in the 2nd century CE or later.

The complex consisted of two palestrae, and its total length was 360 meters. The baths contained typical rooms of the Roman Baths model, such as a changing area, hot, warm, and cold rooms.

The baths were repaired during the reign of Constantine II (337-361), so they are also known as the Constantine Baths.

The harbour baths are presumed to be the stage of the meeting between the heretic Cerinthus and the Apostle John. As Eusebius explains in "Church History": "And there are those that heard from him that John, the disciple of the Lord, going to bathe in Ephesus and seeing Cerinthus within, ran out of the bath-house without bathing, crying, 'Let us flee, lest even the bath fall, because Cerinthus, the enemy of the truth, is within.'"

Another one of the fascinating histories related to Ephesus is linked with an inscription found in the harbour quarter, on the underside of a marble lintel of a building. This so-called Ephesian Abgar Inscription dates back to the 5th or the 6th century CE, and it contains the text of a letter that Jesus supposedly wrote to Abgar, king of Edessa in Syria. Abgar V is claimed to be one of the first Christian kings in history, and the church historian Eusebius recorded the existence in the Edessan archives of a copy of the correspondence exchanged between Abgar of Edessa and Jesus.

However, many modern scholars treat this story only as a genealogical myth. The Abgar Inscription contains the text of a letter from Jesus to Abgar who invited him to cure his illness. Jesus declined the invitation but promised to send someone else instead. The original inscription is now in the Ephesus Museum in Vienna, but several copies exist, including one in the Ephesus Museum in Selçuk and one in the Ashmolean Museum in Oxford.

Great Theatre

GPS coordinates: 37.941419, 27.342517

The grand theatre of Ephesus is a splendidly preserved and imposing building. This structure, the largest in Ephesus, was built entirely of marble. It has a width of 145 meters, its audience is up to 30 meters high, and it could once accommodate around 20,000-25,000 people. Towering above the city, the theatre provided spectacular views, especially of the harbour quarter. It was also one of the first sights that the visitors arriving at the centre of Ephesus could glimpse when following the Arcadiane Street. However, the theatre had begun its existence as a much smaller structure than the one we can see today.

The construction of the theatre began in the Hellenistic times, taking advantage of the natural slope of the Pion Hill (Panayır Dağ) that supported the auditorium. Possibly, the first theatre had already existed when Lysimachus refunded Ephesus in the 3rd century BCE. However, the orchestra with the drainage channel and the lower sectors of seats date back to the 1st century BCE.

This first theatre most probably had a cavea with a single tier of seats, an orchestra with a drainage channel, and a simple one-story stage house (skene). This building was more modest in size from the theatre that can still be seen today, but its dimensions were also impressive. Its skene building was around 41 meters long and 11 meters wide. This makes the Hellenistic theatre of Ephesus one of the largest such structures in Asia Minor of that period. Our knowledge of this earlier theatre comes from the discovered fragments of the Hellenistic skene.

Great theatre with three tiers of seats visible

Renovations of the theatre were initiated in the Roman period, during the reign of Emperor Claudius (41-54 CE). The theatre was enlarged, and the two-storey skene, the structure at the back of a stage, was built during the reign of Emperor Nero (54-68 CE). The façade of the skene was beautifully decorated with aediculae (niches for statues) and columns on two levels. The completion of this project took place only in the times of Emperor Trajan (98-117 CE).

The final result was the theatre with the upper, middle, and lower seating areas separated by diazomata (passages in the auditorium), but it is still unclear when the theatre attained the third level of seating. The shape of the audience section exceeded a semicircle.

The legs of the seats were in the shape of lion's paws, as it can still be seen today. There was also a box reserved for the emperors, and its ceiling coffer lies in the orchestra, but its original location remains unknown. The highest part of the auditorium was completed with a colonnade. Vaulted substructures supported the outer sides of the auditorium.

Furthermore, the skene building had three levels and five doors with the middle one larger than the others. A bust or a statue of the emperor stood in the niche over this central door. In front of the skene, at the height of 2.5 metres above the ground floor, there was a podium used by the actors. Thus, the theatre of Ephesus was one of the largest theatres of the ancient world.

In ancient times, with no electricity available to amplify the sound, it was necessary to use other methods so that the numerous audience of the theatre could hear what was said or sung on the scene. First of all, the shape of the theatre itself was crucial – by clearing the view, the sound could be transmitted further. For this purpose, very steep tiers of seats were necessary, and the angle of the slope increased with the distance.

Secondly, the material from which the seats were made had a filtering effect, suppressing low frequencies of sounds and minimizing background noises of the crowd. Finally, the ancient expert on architecture, Vitruvius, explained that the theatres in Anatolia were equipped with clay or bronze vessels placed around the cavea to help improve acoustics.

The concerts still are organised in the theatre of Ephesus, attracting such artists as Elton John, Mikis Theodorakis, Ray Charles, Sting, and Diana Ross. These events provide an excellent opportunity to test the outstanding acoustics of the theatre and offer an unforgettable experience for the spectators.

Sitting in the ancient seats of the Ephesus theatre is an exceptional opportunity to imagine how the ancient Ephesians may have enjoyed the performances. The best seats were the ones in the front rows, with special places reserved for the most prominent citizens. Those less fortunate could use 58 staircases to get to their seats. As the steepness of the rows increases with the height, those sitting at the back of the theatre could still get an unobstructed view.

The theatre was never covered with a roof, but an awning protected the audience against the sun or rain. A high wall around the orchestra was added in the 4th century to protect the people in the lowest seats from injuries during the fights of gladiators and wild animals.

In the early 2nd century CE, the Aristion (Kaystros) aqueduct was built, to supply the Trajan Nymphaeum. Its course made it necessary to construct a channel through the upper section of the theatre. This modification can be seen today at the 8th seating row of the middle tier.

The theatre was used for many kinds of events: dramatic performances, concerts, artistic and sports competitions. In the Roman period, it was also used, along with the stadium, as the place of gladiatorial combats. Finally, it served the citizens as the meeting place of the ekklesia, i.e. the popular assembly that gathered annually.

The theatre was also an essential element of the cult of Artemis of Ephesus, as it was the point where the procession from the Artemision made one of the stops. Furthermore, it was close to the Commercial Agora, where the silversmiths who produced votive statues of the goddess worked and traded their wares. The theatre became famous during St. Paul's stay in Ephesus when the silversmiths revolted against his teachings, and a vast crowd gathered in the theatre.

The building was partly destroyed by the earthquake that struck the city in the 3rd century. Nevertheless, the structure continued to serve its original purposes. Other earthquakes, in the 4th century, further damaged the audience. In the Byzantine period, in the 8th century, the building was incorporated into the city's defensive fortification system and lost its original significance.

The theatre was first excavated in the 19th century. The initial investigations were carried out by J. T. Wood in the period from 1863 and 1874. However, the structure was wholly excavated only 30 years later, by the Austrian Archaeological Institute. After a break of almost 100 years, new excavations and studies began in the 1990s.

The theatre underwent many renovations and partial reconstructions, and no all the decisions related to these processes were fortunate. For instance, the cement-based mortar was used as its harmful effects were unknown. Recent conservation activities have been focused on the removal of this mortar and the increasing of the visibility of original materials.

A humble structure of the Hellenistic Fountain is located in the north-western corner of the back wall of the theatre's skene building. The fountain, placed between two columns in the Ionic order, faces the courtyard in front of the theatre. The elegant proportions and the style of its stone ornaments suggest that the structure dates back to the Hellenistic times, that is, to the 3rd or the 2nd century BCE. Water was collected in the pool in front of the fountain, from the taps in the shape of lions' mouths.

The fountain was expanded in the 4th century CE, when two new massive columns without flutes were put in front of the two slender Ionic columns, creating the new anteroom, two-meters-deep. An inscription on one of these new columns informs us that the water collected there was brought from the Marnas River (now called Dervenddere). The restoration of the structure was completed in 1990. The pool nearby belongs to another fountain built at a later period, but the basin of the Hellenistic Fountain has not been preserved.

If the views from the top seats of the theatre were stunning, just imagine what kind of vistas could be enjoyed by the inhabitants of a luxurious residence erected higher on the slopes of Panayır Dağ. Indeed, there are the remains of a splendid villa above the theatre. Naturally, such an important house in the commanding location must have belonged to someone holding immense power, but his identity remains unknown. Unfortunately, the mansion is off-limits to visitors, at least for now.

Commercial Agora

GPS coordinates: 37.940020, 27.340650

The Commercial (Lower) Agora of Ephesus was linked to the harbour by the Arcadiane, and stood close to its junction with the Marble Street, just to the south-west of the theatre. With its almost square plan, the Tetragonos Agora — whose ancient name, meaning the Square Market, has been confirmed by the inscriptions — was built for commercial purposes.

It had impressive dimensions, as its sides were 111 meters long. The Commercial Agora had three main gates, enabling access from the north onto Harbour Street, from the south-east, and from the west. The most impressive and best-preserved of these gates is the so-called Gate of Mazaeus and Mithridates on the south-eastern side of the agora, very close to the Celsus Library.

The Commercial Agora as the trade area was established in Ephesus in the Hellenistic times, in the 3rd century BCE, as evidenced by the western gate fragments in the Ionic order. The agora's location was carefully selected, close to the harbour and over a spacious area. As the land was not completely flat there, the ground must have been levelled when it was constructed.

However, the place where the agora was created had been in use for a much longer time. Interestingly, the excavations carried out since 1987 on the western side of the Commercial Agora brought to light the evidence of an early settlement, belonging to Archaic Ephesus, now lying six metres below the ground. The archaeologists hypothesize that these could be the traces of the Smyrna quarter of the city, mentioned by Strabo: "[...] for the Ephesians were fellow-inhabitants of the Smyrnaeans in ancient times, when Ephesus was also called Smyrna. [...] Smyrna was an Amazon who took possession of Ephesus; and hence the name both of the inhabitants and of the city".

The archaeologists revealed five successive building phases, reaching back to the 8th century BCE. These buildings were erected on stone foundations with clay walls, evolving from single-room structures, into large residential houses. They were abandoned by the mid-6th century BCE, possibly because of the rising sea level. In the 6th century BCE, a pottery kiln was erected within these ruined residences. The industrial activities in the western part of the agora continued until the early 4th century BCE. On the opposite, eastern side of the agora, the excavations revealed a graveyard from the period of 6th to 4th centuries BCE.

The Commercial Agora was surrounded by colonnaded porticoes, significantly enhanced during the Roman period. The agora was restructured many times, firstly in the 1st century BCE, when it acquired its square shape. This Hellenistic Agora, excavated in 1977, was three meters lower than the current ground level. The archaeologists found a warehouse from the 3rd century BCE in the southwestern corner, a stoa behind it, and the colonnades near the western gate.

The modifications to the plan of the agora were introduced during the reign of Emperor Augustus. By that time, the stoas surrounding the agora had two floors, as indicated by the remains of the staircases discovered in several places. Behind the colonnades, there were around 100 rooms that mainly served as shops but were also used as workshops, warehouses, and meeting places for guild associations.

The colonnades surrounding the agora on four sides were decorated with hundreds of statues of orators, philosophers, athletes, and officials. Only their foundations have been preserved, including the inscriptions that provide valuable information about the social life in Ephesus. The Augustan Agora was severely damaged by an earthquake around 23 CE. It was quickly reconstructed

Corinthian columns still standing on the Commercial Agora

and was in operation 20 years later when the statue of Emperor Claudius was sponsored by the Roman merchants.

Not all merchants and artisans who used to work in the Commercial Agora remain anonymous. Possibly, the best-known of them is St. Paul, who worked there with Priscilla and Aquila in their tent making and leather working business. Their history is mentioned in the Acts: "There [in Corinth] he met a Jew named Aquila, a native of Pontus, who had recently come from Italy with his wife Priscilla, because Claudius had ordered all Jews to leave Rome. [...] and because he was a tentmaker as they were, he stayed and worked with them." It must have been a lucrative enterprise as the Romans used leather products widely — from clothing such as heavy raincoats worn by the soldiers, through harnesses and shields, to footwear. Asia Minor was one of the chief sources of leather for the Romans, who needed enormous quantities of this material.

St. Paul also got in trouble there as he criticised the local silversmiths who sold the miniature silver shrines of Artemis. St. Paul denounced their activity as idolatry and, as a result, was forced to hastily leave the city. The closeness of the Commercial Agora to the harbour may have even been the reason why St. Paul avoided visiting Ephesus on the way to Jerusalem, as described in the Acts 20:16: "Paul had decided to sail past Ephesus to avoid spending time in the province of Asia, for he was in a hurry to reach Jerusalem, if possible, by the day of Pentecost."

During the reign of Emperor Nero, a two-storied double Doric basilica, 150 meters long, was added on the eastern side of the Commercial Agora, along the Marble Street. It was originally intended as a justice court. It is now known as the Hall of Nero, because of the inscription that dedicated this building to Artemis, Nero, his mother Agrippina, and the Ephesians. The basilica was later modified, and its front, facing Marble Street, was closed off, leaving only a small entrance on the northern side.

Extensive restorations of the Commercial Agora were carried out in the times of Emperor Caracalla, at the beginning of the 3rd century when new two-aisled stoas were erected. The agora was damaged by an earthquake again, in the late 4th century CE. Then it was repaired during the reign of Emperor Theodosius I. In this restoration, all the main structural elements of the square were repaired, utilizing the architectural pieces collected throughout Ephesus.

In the 6th century CE, the northern stoa of the agora was rebuilt as a massive retaining wall, supporting the artificial hill behind it. The agora remained in use until as late as the 7th century CE, keeping its general plan. However, it lost its original function and was used as a space for workshops, such a glass-makers.

The so-called horologion, a combination of solar and water clock, stood at the centre of the Agora. In its original sense, an horologion — from the Greek word meaning "the hour-teller" — was any device for keeping time. The excellent example of such horologion is the Tower of the Winds in Athens that was also a combination of sundials and a water clock. In the case of the horologion of Ephesus, it was discovered as the foundations of the building, measuring some 10 to 6 meters. The archaeologists assumed that it belonged to the horologion based on late Hellenistic inscriptions. However, later studies demonstrated that this structure was from a much later period, i.e from the 6th century CE.

Gate of Mazaeus and Mithridates

GPS coordinates: 37.939261, 27.341019

The Commercial Agora had three main gates. The most impressive and best-preserved of them is the south-eastern one, called the Gate of Mazaeus and Mithridates. This monument is also the only large-scale structure of the Augustan building programme that survived the earthquake of 23 CE.

The Gate of Mazaeus and Mithridates has three arched openings, and the central opening recedes by 1.5 meters. The gate's façade is beautifully decorated with floral motives. The portal is an excellent example of the donation of a public building by private individuals. The gate features three main inscriptions over its arches: on the sides, there are Latin texts, but the central text is in Greek. They inform that the gate was erected by two freedmen of Octavian Augustus and Marcus Agrippa, called Mazaeus and Mithridates.

As a gravestone found in Ephesus states that Mithridates was the freedman of Agrippa, Mazaeus must have been the one freed by Augustus. Thankful for the manumission, they had this gate built in the honour of Octavian Augustus, his wife Livia, his son-in-law Marcus Agrippa, and Julia the elder, the daughter of Augustus and the wife of Agrippa.

The titles given to Octavian Augustus allowed dating the gate to the years 3-4 BCE. At this time, Agrippa had been dead for nine years and his widow, Julia, remarried to Tiberius. Thus, the inscription, in a delicate diplomatic manoeuvre, calls her "the daughter of Augustus" instead of mentioning her husbands.

Originally, these inscriptions were made of gold-plated bronze

Gate of Mazaeus and Mithridates seen from the Triodos Square

letters, but only their sockets can be seen today. The Latin and Greek versions are different because the Greek text claims that the gate had previously been dedicated to the Ephesian "demos" (the people), while the Latin texts do not use this formula.

The Latin inscription on the left arch mentions Augustus, and the inscription on the right arch is for Agrippa. Each freedman's name is given on the part of the gate dedicated to their patrons, respectively. Moreover, the analyses of the style of the decorations of the left and right parts of the gate indicated that different teams of sculptors had been responsible for their production.

There are additional inscriptions below, informing about commercial regulations in Ephesus, such as price edicts and grain supply. The vault from the side of the Library of Celsus is lined with black marble, in contrast to the vault on the opposite side, lined with white marble. The gate may also have been a memorial monument for Mazaeus and Mithridates who are possibly buried in the annexes of their parts of the gate, as indicated by an inscription found nearby.

Archaeological excavations carried out in the area of the gate offer us an opportunity to conclude that the ancient architects and builders also made mistakes and encountered construction problems. In the case of the gate, it was originally designed to be used by vehicles. Its original floor was on the same level as the Commercial Agora and the square where the Library of Celsus was erected one century later. However, this solution caused the difficulty with the rainwater that flowed freely from the paved square and covered the Commercial Agora with mud. Thus, the need arose to rectify this situation, and a drainage pipe was added below, as discovered in the 1903 excavations. The system of pipes collected the rainwater and transported it to the sea. However, after such additions, the level of the gate floor was raised, and it was no longer possible to pass it in a carriage.

The ancient gates were problematic places to keep clean, as it also happens nowadays. An inscription found near the Gate of Mazaeus and Mithridates informs that "Whoever urinates here will be punished". What kind of punishment was on offer remains a mystery. Obviously, not everyone made it on time to the public latrines or found a bucket that served as a public urinal. The contents of these urinals were collected and bought by the fullers, who used them for cleaning textiles.

The present state of the Gate of Mazaeus and Mithridates is the result of the restoration project that was carried out between 1980 and 1989. Importantly, the southern façade was fully restored with the almost exclusive use of the ancient building materials.

Library of Celsus

GPS coordinates: 37.939209, 27.340901

The Library of Celsus is probably the most distinctive building commonly associated with Ephesus, photographed thousands of times per day. However, this impressive monument erected to honour and bury a prominent politician deserves a much closer look than just another selfie snapped quickly before moving on.

The Library of Celsus takes its name from Tiberius Julius Celsus Polemaenus. He was the Roman governor of Asia Minor at the beginning of the 2nd century CE. More importantly, he was one of the first men of the Greek origins to become the Senator of Rome and to hold high-level offices in the Empire's eastern provinces. It is commonly assumed that he was born in Sardis, and descended from a long line of local nobility and priests. He was also related to other influential eastern senators, including C. Julius Antiochus Epiphanes Philopappus, the grandson of Antiochus IV, the last king of the Commagene Kingdom.

Celsus had a long public career service that ended around 106-107 CE with the position of the Proconsul of the Asia Province. When his term in this office finished, he most probably remained in Ephesus and died there at the age of seventy, before the year 114 CE. He was buried in a garlanded sarcophagus under the library bearing his name. The burial chamber underneath the building also served as a heroon, i.e. a shrine to a hero, making the building a truly unique feature in the classical world, which generally shunned burials within the cities.

Only particularly meritorious citizens could be buried inside public buildings in exceptional instances, and this was the case of Julius Celsus Polemaenus. His skeleton still lies in a lead casket inside the sarcophagus, under the large niche of the vaulted substructure. This sarcophagus was chiselled from a single block of marble and decorated with garlands carried by Eros and Nike. As the sarcophagus is around 2.7 meters long, it must have been brought to the crypt before the library was erected over it, as the passageway leading there is too narrow.

The nature of Celsus' services to Ephesus that earned him the privilege of the intramural burial is unclear. Perhaps Celsus had favoured Ephesus over other cities of Asia Province while holding a position of a proconsul. Quite possibly, he made a promise to adorn the city with a library and donated his books to this purpose. Volker Michael Strocka presents a tempting theory that Celsus was convinced to give his books to the city of Ephesus at the suggestion of the great historian Tacitus who held the position of a proconsul of Asia in 112 or 113 CE. Thus, his stay in Ephesus coincided with the time of Celsus' death.

The sarcophagus of Celsus within the library bearing his name is only one of several examples of intra-urban burials of Ephesus. Like other ancient Greek and Roman cities, Ephesus was surrounded by large-scale necropoleis, and the placement of the cemeteries outside the walls had a long tradition. It could be easily explained, considering sanitary precautions and the fear of the dead. The ban of burials within the settlement is one of the Roman oldest laws, already noted in the Twelve Tables that constituted the foundation of the Roman law.

This ban was only lifted in the 9th century CE when the Christian custom of burials next to the churches within the cities came to the fore. Despite this tradition, the privilege to bury prominent citizens and heroes within the city space had taken place in Ephesus even in the late Hellenistic period. Apart from the Library of Celsus, the burial monuments that also played the role of honorific monuments in Ephesus include the Androklos Heroon, the Octagon, the Memmius Monument, and the Pollio Monument,

Library of Celsus

all situated along Curetes Street.

The Library of Celsus itself was also an unusual monument, as it was among the first private-endowed public libraries in the classical ancient world and one of the earliest such buildings dedicated to an individual who was not of royal descent. Until its erection, most other ancient buildings that have been identified as public libraries were built by kings or emperors.

Its construction began in 110 CE as the building was intended as a kind of mausoleum donated by Celsus' son, Titus Julius Aquila Polemaeanus. He also left a bequest of 25,000 denarii, of which 8% was to be used for the purchase of books, the coronation of the statues, and the sacred ceremonies connected with the cult of the dead. His descendants finished the construction of the library in 135 CE. Inscriptions of the building also inform us about Celsus' career and describe annual festivals to be held in his honour.

Although it were the Romans who invented the bound books as we know them, the majority of the works collected in the Celsus Library were in the form of scrolls. They were written on parchment or papyrus, and the readers unrolled and then re-rolled the fragment they wanted to read. The multi-volume scrolls were stored in leather buckets with a tagged spindle indicating the title. In the Library of Celsus, two rows of niches, located on the inner sides of the walls of the building, can be seen. It is known that originally there was the third row. The manuscripts were stored on shelves placed in these niches.

It is frequently said that the library boasted a vast collection of 12,000 scrolls, and this number would have made it the third-richest library in ancient times after the ones in Alexandria and Pergamon. However, this number is just a result of theoretical calculations of the potential space for the books, and there are no literary sources to confirm it. It is even unclear whether the shelves and cabinets of the library were all full of scrolls.

The access to the scrolls placed on the upper floors was provided by a two-storey gallery running along three sides of the library. The largest, central niche, decorated with a big arch, served as the place where the statue of Celsus or of the goddess Athena, as it was the case of the library in Pergamon, once stood.

The two-story structure of the library was supported by four pairs of columns, between which there were three entrances to the building. The columns of the lower level are of Corinthian order, while the ones on the upper level have composite capitals. Three windows were placed at the level of the second floor, illuminating the reading room and taking advantage of the best light from the east. At the same time, this orientation protected the contents of the library from the moist sea winds from the west, as there were no openings on the western rear wall.

The building was erected from the best materials available. The column shafts, all made from single blocks, were carved from honey-coloured marble from Synnada, an ancient town of Phrygia Salutaris. Other architectural pieces were made of while Ephesian marble. Nine steps lead into the library, and the building rises to the height of 17 meters, while it is 21 meters wide.

The statues adorning the façade of the Library of Celsus represent the Four Virtues or the Hellenic cultural values of Celsus: Sophia (Wisdom), Arete (Competence or Bravery), Episteme (Knowledge or Understanding), and Ennoia (Thought or Inspiration). Originally, all these statues were made of bronze, as indicated by the traces on the plinths. However, they were, most possibly, melted down after the fire of the library in the 3rd century. Some time afterwards, they were replaced with female marble statues, evidently acquired from some ruined buildings in Ephesus. Unfortunately, the statues that can be seen in Ephesus today are just the modern-day copies, as the originals are in the Ephesos Museum in Vienna.

All these statues, made of marble, were found in the debris in front of the Library of Celsus. Only two of them, representing Sophia and Arete, kept their heads. The statue of Sophia is a Roman copy from the 1st half of the 2nd century CE, made after an earlier Hellenistic model. This robed statue of a Greek goddess is of the type known as the Hellenistic Hera Campana. It was repurposed by adding an inscription on the plinth: the Greek words identify her as the personification of the Wisdom of Celsus, the library's patron.

The Hellenistic female statue from the 1st century BCE was repurposed as the personification of Competence (Greek — Arete, Latin — Virtus). This virtue was one of the most cherished character traits of a Roman citizen. The female is wearing a delicate robe and a serpent bracelet, typical of an honorary statue. Its head, from the Antonine portrait of the 2nd century CE, was separately made and then attached to the body.

The statue repurposed to represent Episteme is a Roman portrait statue type from the 2nd century CE. It has an artfully draped robe that was originally pulled over the head. The scholars claim that it was a personification of Celsus' Understanding, based on the knowledge obtained from the books in the library.

The fourth statue, representing Ennoia (Inspiration) is a Roman copy, made in the 2nd century CE, after a Hellenistic model. The torso of this female statue is of a type popular for the goddess Ceres. It is even possible to reconstruct the attribute in her raised right hand: she once held an ear of corn or a torch. The statue was repurposed for a personification of the Inspiration, but there is an element of surprise, based on the inscription placed on its plinth. First of all, the inscription on the plinth is the only one of the four statues not incised but painted. Moreover, the other three inscriptions clearly refer to Celsus with the second lines adding the word KELSOU to the name of the virtue. Amazingly, the statue of Inspiration was to represent the virtue of otherwise anonymous Philippus (FILIPPOU). The scholars speculate that this statue was to honour the person in charge of administering the donation to restore the façade of the library and who had the inspiration to undertake it.

Other statues were also discovered within the library, one showing a bearded man in military dress, possibly Celsus himself, and another one — of Melpomene, the Muse of Tragedy. However, their original placement is uncertain.

The splendidly decorated façade of the library stands in stark contrast with the modest dimensions of the main and only room of the building, measuring 14.5 to 9.5 meters. There is only an apse, in the centre of the back wall. It is often said that the building was deliberately surrounded by an additional wall, offering adequate protection from moisture for the valuable scrolls. However, the scholar responsible for the reconstruction of the building, Volker Michael Strocka, claims that it is not valid. These walls were not the outer walls of the library, but they simply belonged to adjoining buildings.

The case of the Celsus Library also offers the opportunity to present the ingenuity of ancient architects who were limited by the space available. As the library was a new addition to the already existing buildings, for instance, the Hellenistic-era peristyle house to its south, it had to be squeezed in. As the sponsor expected certain grandeur, the designers had to apply several visual tricks that involved the perspective. The columns, for example, were designed in the way that made the front of the library seem wider than it actually is. The podium that supports the columns is higher in its centre and has lower sides. The capitals of the columns were made smaller than it was usually practised. Moreover, the number of column pairs was reduced, making the building also seem higher than it really is.

The interior of the library, including all the books, was destroyed by fire, which left the façade undamaged. It is not known what exactly had happened, but around 400 CE the library no longer functioned. Quite possibly, it stopped playing the role of a library much earlier, in the earthquake of the 262 CE or when the Goths invaded the city around 268 CE, as there are no records that the building was restored afterwards.

Some parts of the monument continued to be used. First, the interior became a courtyard of a residential property. Next, the area in front of it was turned into a pool, which reflected the beautiful façade, and the whole structure had a purely decorative function. The façade was painted white and decorated with marble statues, randomly brought there from other locations within the city. Three entrances were walled up, and the main hall filled with rubble.

The person responsible for this transformation was the proconsul Stephanus, according to an inscription, beginning and ending with crosses. It has been suggested that he was the same Stephanus who is depicted in the marble statue that is now in the Ephesus Museum in Selçuk. However, the dates do not confirm this connection, as the statue is from the 6th century and thus much younger than the pool. Anyway, Stephanus was a common name then, and the inscription may be referring to the architect of the nymphaeum rather than its sponsor.

The fountain and its façade were finally destroyed by an earthquake in the 10th or the 11th century CE. The wonderful fact is that almost all fragments were preserved, enabling the reconstruction of the building in the 20th century. This signifies that this area of Ephesus remained uninhabited after the earthquake, and the architectural fragments were not reused or burned for lime.

The pieces of the Celsus Library were first unearthed in 1903 by an Austrian archaeologist, Rudolf Heberdey. The excavations continued in 1904, but then were halted for more than sixty years. The stone blocks of the building were stored on the nearby Upper Agora. As early as 1908, the architect Wilhelm Wilberg presented the proposal for the building's reconstruction, on the basis of exact measurements of these fragments.

The façade of the library was reconstructed by an Austrian archaeology foundation in the 1970s from more than 750 fragments found during the excavations. The archaeologists happily realised that some 80% of the original façade still survived in the fragments scattered on the ground. Thus, from 1973 to 1978, the library was reconstructed, with initial funding from the building firm of Hochtief Essen but mostly by a private individual, Anton Kallinger-Prskawetz. He also funded the reconstruction of the Gate of Mazaeus and Mithridates of the Commercial Agora. His name is now commemorated by the street in the centre of the town of Selçuk.

The reconstruction was led by the German archaeologist Volker Michael Strocka. Because many architectural elements of the library had been moved to the museums in Vienna and Istanbul, it was necessary to replace them with copies. Since the reconstruction, the Library of Celsus has been one of the most widely recognised ancient monuments, not only from Ephesus but the whole of Asia Minor. Thus, it is difficult to believe that it had been almost completely demolished and hidden under the debris of Ephesus for several hundred years.

At the site of the monumental pool in front of the Celsus Library, archaeologists have found gigantic reliefs depicting the military victory, most possibly of Marcus Aurelius and Lucius Verus over the Parthians. Therefore, the monument is most commonly known as the Parthian Monument. The reliefs of this monumental structure were found in front of the library, arranged as a basin of the fountain, in front of the outer staircase of the former library. The extant tablets and reliefs of the monument were discovered by the Austrian archaeologists during the first decade of their excavations at Ephesus. This is the reason why almost all pieces of the Parthian Monument are now in the Ephesos Museum in Vienna. The plaster casts of the reliefs, discovered in the 1960s and 1970s, were added later. The originals of these few reliefs are on display in the Ephesus Museum in Selçuk.

Triodos Square

GPS coordinates: 37.939088, 27.341161

Following the Marble (Theatre) Street to the south, the ancient visitors and the modern-era tourists arrive at the very heart of Ephesus, known as Triodos Square. Even today, the moment when one enters the square can take the breath away. To the west, the magnificent façade of the Celsus Library towers over the space. Moreover, previously hidden from the view, the Curetes Street leading to the Upper City becomes visible. To the east, the colonnades gently made a curve and helped to hide the structures behind, including a large peristyle villa and a public latrine.

The name of the square, Triodos, means "Three Roads", as it marked the crossroads of Curetes, Marble, and Ortygia Roads. In this place, the road leading to Ortygia, a sacred groove, believed to be the birthplace of Artemis, started. Initially, the Gate of Mazaeus and Mithridates was erected in the role of the Triodos Gate, at the junction where the Via Sacra (Ortygia Road) to the legendary birthplace of the city's patron deity started. When this section of Ephesus was remodelled, the beginning of the Ortygia Road was moved up the slope to the south and marked with the new Triodos Gate, set at a different angle from the orientation of the three crossing streets.

The new Triodos Gate is now frequently called the Hadrian's Gate. Once, it had three storeys, of which only the lowest one has been preserved. Three openings led through the gate, and the middle one was the widest, with an arched vault. The side openings are still topped by architraves. The whole structure resembles the

The new Triodos Gate also called the Hadrian's Gate

Arch of Hadrian in Athens and was thus dubbed the Hadrian's Gate. The building was restored after an earthquake in 262 CE, and water basins were added to its sides.

However, the gate was probably erected earlier, during the reign of Emperor Trajan, most likely as a triumphal monument. Its great dimensions suggest that it may also have been used for religious and ceremonial purposes. This assumption is strengthened by the gate's specific location. At the junction marked by the gate, a statue of Artemis once stood. Its fate is recorded in the inscription found nearby. It states that a person called Demeas tore it down as the image of "demon Artemis". He replaced it with a cross, the symbol of Jesus Christ. This event happened sometime in the early Christian era.

Nowadays, the gate, one of the most excellent examples of the sumptuous marble carvings of the period of Trajan and Hadrian, marks the location of the entry to the Terrace Houses. The gate's partial restoration was carried out between 1986 and 1990 by the Austrian Institute of Archaeology, financed by Anton Kallinger-Prskawetz.

Just to the right of the Hadrian's Gate, another important monument was situated. It was an altar dating back to the early imperial period. Its exact function remains the subject of the scholarly debate. The visible remains consist of a broad stairway that connects the U-shaped loggia with the Triodos Square. Peter Scherrer suggested that it was once the foundation of the so-called Parthian Monument, later reused for the pool in front of the Celsus Library.

However, Friedmund Hueber proposed that this open structure could serve the jurisdiction purposes. If it was the case, the stairs could function as seats for the audience following the court proceedings. Finally, Dieter Knibbe concentrated on the sacred function of the area and suggested that the structure was the altar to Artemis. If the structure was decorated with the Parthian Monument, it could be considered a memorial to Emperor Lucius Verus with respect to the city's chief deity.

The traces of a structure erected on the circular plan, to the right of the Gate of Mazaeus and Mithridates and opposite the Hadrian's (Triodos) Gate, belong to the so-called Circular Monument with a Fountain. It stood in front of the southern end of the Hall of Nero. Some researchers such as Hueber believe that this building, formerly a six-columned monopteros with Corinthian capitals and a conical roof, was the horologion, relocated here from the Commercial Agora. Other scholars, for instance Scherrer, state that it was a decorative fountain, beautifully contrasting with the simple façade of the Hall of Nero behind it.

Public latrines

GPS coordinates: 37.938910, 27.341604

In the quarter of Ephesus located to the north-east of the junction of Marble and Curetes streets, a public latrine was found. It was constructed in the 1st century CE over a channel with an uninterrupted flow of water. The toilet seats were formed by cutting holes into marble benches that line the walls, and their total number was 48. There were three rows of toilets along three sides of the latrine.

In the centre, there was an uncovered pool that collected rainwater and provided refreshment in the hot days of summer. The clients were protected from rain by a wooden roof supported by the columns surrounding the pool. The floor was covered with a mosaic. The public latrines were erected as a part of a larger building scheme — of the so-called Scholastica Baths that provided grey water for flushing the toilets. In winter, the latrines were kept warm by an underground heating system that funnelled steam from the baths.

In the ancient cities of the Roman period, most of the inhabitants did not have a luxury of a private bathroom or toilet. This privilege was limited to the most prominent and wealthy citizens, such as the owners of splendid villas situated on the slope of the hill opposite to the public latrines, or the bishop of Ephesus who had a grand residence built for him in the vicinity of the Church of Mary. However, the vast majority of the Ephesians had to use public toilets on a regular basis. The whole idea of using the toilet in a company of strangers might be shocking to many modern visitors,

Public latrines, partly reconstructed

but it was standard practice in the cities of the Roman Empire.

Probably nothing worked better to diminish the perception of one's status and importance than the necessity to use the public latrine — in the company of several dozens of other clients. The latrines were actually a meeting place, to chat and exchange gossip and news. Surprisingly for the modern tastes, the latrines were actually quite comfortable places, where people spent a lot of time, reading, thinking, or begging the dinner invitations as in the famous ditty by Martial indicates: "Why does Vacerra spend his hours in all the privies, and day-long stoop? He wants a supper, not a poop."

As there was no toilet paper available in the Roman period, the issue of getting clean after using the restroom naturally arose. The clients used sponges attached to sticks that were stored in vinegar for hygienic purposes and washed in the channel with clean running water after each use. Sounds disgusting, does it not? Let's just add that to keep the seats warm, public slaves were sitting there, waiting for the customers. It is an excellent illustration of how different was the idea of privacy and personal hygiene two thousand years ago.

The latrines of Ephesus were also studied by archaeologists and biologists who were interested in the hygienic conditions and parasite infections in the Roman period. They analysed the mineralized faecal material from a private house latrine, the sewer drain of a public communal latrine, and sediment from the harbour canal. The results demonstrated that the inhabitants of ancient Ephesus suffered from the parasites, as eggs of roundworm were found in the public latrine, whipworm in the house latrine, and both whipworm and roundworm in the harbour canal. Surprisingly, considering the unique position of Ephesus as the capital of Asia Province and huge trading harbour, there was a lack of diversity in parasite species found. It is essential to mention that these parasites were spread by the contamination of food and drink by human faeces. Thus, it appears that the ancient Ephesians did not always wash their hands before cooking and eating.

Scholastica Baths

GPS coordinates: 37.938727, 27.342042

The large building of the so-called Scholastica Baths, discovered in Ephesus in 1926, was constructed in the late first or the early second century CE. P. Quintilius Valens Varius originally built the baths, and hence the structure is sometimes referred to as the Varius Baths.

However, the remains that we can see today are from the 4th century CE, when a Christian woman named Scholastica carried out the renovation project. Her seated, headless statue still decorates a niche in the apodyterium, i.e. the changing room in ancient Roman public baths.

The baths are separated from the latrines and the residential houses by a narrow lane called Academy Street, leading down from the north slope of Panayırdağ. There are two entrances, one from this street and another — from the Curetes Street. The visit to the Scholastica Baths offers a chance to understand the bathing habits of the ancient Ephesians. As only the wealthiest homes were equipped with private baths, the vast majority of the inhabitants of the city had to use public baths instead.

In ancient times, the visit to the baths was a part of the daily routine. Men and women usually bathed separately — in the same baths but at different times of the day. The visit was not only the occasion to get clean, but also to relax, get a massage, and exchange information and gossip.

The Scholastica Baths are an excellent illustration of how elaborated the Roman baths could be — their plan was far more ad-

Statue of Scholastica decorating the baths

vanced than the one of a simple bathroom. The original structure was thought to have been three-storied, but the upper two stories collapsed. The plan of the ground floor follows a typical Roman-era bathhouse.

First, the visitors entered the dressing room (apodyterium), then — the cold room (frigidarium) with the pool, followed by the warm room (tepidarium) to relax, and finally — the hot room (caldarium) with an elaborate heating system. The ceramic fragments of the hypocaust system that heated the floors of the baths can still be seen there. The main architectural style of the modified structure is very similar to the original form from the 1st century CE.

Curetes Street

GPS coordinates: 37.938522, 27.341797

Curetes Street is one of the main thoroughfares of Ephesus. It leads from the Library of Celsus to the Hercules Gate, extending along a northwest-southeast axis, in the saddle between the Panayir and Bülbül hills. Curetes Street can be considered the link between two main areas of Ephesus — the political and the commercial one. After leaving the Lower (Commercial) Agora, the walk uphill along this street takes the visitors to the vicinity of the Upper (State) Agora, the political heart of ancient Ephesus.

Its strategic location meant that Curetes Street's role was not only purely practical as the communication link between two parts of Ephesus. It was also a part of the processional route that was followed to celebrate the city's chief goddess, Artemis. Finally, similarly to the Arcadiane, Curetes Street played the role of an ostentatious boulevard, created to impress the visitors and show off the wealth of Ephesus.

In antiquity the street was most possibly called Embolos, literally meaning a wedge, as this name is mentioned not only in literary sources but also confirmed by the inscriptions discovered in the area of the street and the Commercial Agora. This name could be the reflection of the street's location, as it was wedged in the narrow valley between two hills. Thus, the street did not follow the orthogonal grid plan of the Greco-Roman city, as instead the shape of the valley dictated its course.

The name used currently, Curetes Street, comes from the priests called the Curetes, who took care of the flame of the Prytaneion where their names were written down. The column drums from the Prytaneion, covered with lists of the cult association of the Curetes, were reused in the lower north colonnade of the street where they were discovered by archaeologists.

Astonishingly, this street was used for a thousand years at least, as evidenced by the excavations. The earliest archaeological traces of the street date back to the 3rd century BCE. In this period, the lower Embolos consisted of a gravel road that was later delimited by a curb. In the Roman period, the street was paved with marble stones for the first time.

Along Curetes Street there were once fountains, statues, and shops, of which those located on the southern side had two storeys. The street also had a well-developed sewer system underneath. The street was originally 210 meters long, and from 6.8 to 10 meters wide. It is rather steep, with the elevation of around 20 meters, and it climbs from the Triodos Square in the direction of the State Agora.

The street was frequently damaged by the earthquakes, for instance in the 3rd and 4th centuries CE. For that reason, the buildings along Curetes Street were repeatedly damaged and then underwent refurbishment. After the earthquake in the 4th century CE, the collapsed columns were replaced by others, collected from the various areas of the city, including the ones taken from the Prytaneion. The resulting confusion of architectural styles can be seen to this day.

In the early Byzantine period, Ephesus underwent a construction boom, resulting from renewed prosperity of the city. In these times, also Curetes Street was refurbished, including the restoration and reconstruction of the monumental fountains situated at the lower section of the street. At the same time, the street was closed to traffic when the Hercules Gate was erected on its eastern end. The street continued to function until the 6th or even the 7th century CE as the archaeologists found taverns and workshops of the craftsman quarter from this period in the areas bordering the street.

Curetes Street with the Terraced Houses to the left

The visitors starting their walk down Curetes Street from the Triodos Square encounter a group of buildings lining the street to the south. The proximity to the so-called Hadrian's Gate and the monumental staircase that possibly was the Altar of Artemis signifies their importance. This group consists of three structures, from the west to the east: the Hellenistic Heroon, the Octagon, and the Hexagon. In their background, there are the so-called Terrace Houses, the built-up residential area on the northern slope of Bülbüldağ Hill.

HELLENISTIC HEROON

The first of these three structures is the Hellenistic Heroon, frequently referred to as the Androklos Heroon. The remains of this building that resembles a pool stand at the south-western ending of Curetes Street. The heroon — a sanctuary dedicated to a hero — was built in the Hellenistic period, in the 2nd century BCE. It was a U-shaped structure with a Doric façade on a ground floor and an open upper level of the Ionic order. In front of the building, there is a water basin, as it later served as a fountain. The enclosure panels were renovated in the late ancient times when cross reliefs were added. Therefore, the monument was known as the Byzantine Fountain for a long time, and even today, many visitors believe that it is a Christian monument.

The key element that enabled the researchers to provide an interpretation of this heroon was the relief from its pediment. It shows a figure of a horseman dressed in a short chiton (a kind of tunic that fastens at the shoulder) with a chlamys (a type of ancient Greek cloak) unfurling backwards. The whole relief presented a battle between a horseman and a hoplite, a charioteer, a fallen figure in heroic nakedness, and armed warriors.

One of the ancient authors, Pausanias, informs us about the fate of the legendary founder of Ephesus, Androklos: "But after that the Samians had returned to their own land, Androklos helped the people of Priene against the Carians. The Greek army was victorious, but Androklos was killed in the battle. The Ephesians carried off his body and buried it in their own land, at the spot where his tomb is pointed out at the present day, on the road leading from the sanctuary past the Olympieum to the Magnesian gate. On the tomb is a statue of an armed man."

This information, along with the frieze, led many researchers to believe that the battle for the fallen figure may illustrate the heroic death of Androklos. As the founder of Ephesus, he may have been buried not outside the city, but in its very centre, where his grave provided protection against the enemies. Possibly, the statue of Androklos stood on the upper floor of the Heroon as its base with a dedication to this hero as ktistes (meaning a founder) was discovered nearby.

However, the identification of the Heroon building located at the western end of Curetes Street with the grave of Androklos is very uncertain. If Androklos had ever existed, he could have been interred inside or outside the city, as the burial laws or customs from this early period of history (the end of the 11th century BCE) are unknown. Moreover, most scholars accept that the early Ionian settlement was situated near Ayasoluk Hill and not between Pion (Panayır Dağ) and Koressos (Bülbül Dağ) hills. Thus, the location of the so-called Androklos Heroon does not make much sense in this context. Moreover, the structure did not contain a burial chamber, so possibly it was not even a funerary monument. Finally, while some scholars such as Hilke Thür drew the connection between the building and the legendary Hypelaia spring, the fountain was actually fed by a canal and not by a spring.

Interestingly, the archaeologists found a sarcophagus on the western side of the so-called Androklos Heroon. Inside, there was a skeleton of a 60-70-year-old man with a marble portrait of an Imperial priest. The sarcophagus dates back to the end of the 1st century CE or the beginning of the 2nd century CE, and it is possibly the resting place of certain Tiberius Claudius Aristion, the founder of the Trajan Nymphaeum. His sarcophagus was perhaps moved to this new location in Late Antiquity.

Octagon

Next to the Hellenistic Heroon, stands another burial monument, known as the Octagon. Dating back to the late 1st century BCE, this building was a monumental eight-sided mausoleum, around 13 meters high, originally surrounded by a Corinthian colonnade, standing on a square base with the sides 9 meters long. It was covered, most possibly, with a steep pyramidal roof, a novel architectural solution at the time. All visible parts were made of white marble.

Today, not much can be seen of the original octagonal building. Only its square pedestal is still standing on the Curetes Street, while many fragments are in the storage of the excavation site. However, two columns and some pieces of the cornice were removed to Austria in the early 20th century and are now on display in the Ephesos Museum in Vienna.

The Octagon was discovered in 1904, and it was first interpreted as a trophy-monument. However, further excavations, carried out in 1929, found a burial chamber situated on the top of the basal structure. Inside, there was a sarcophagus with the skeleton of a young woman of 15–18 years at the time of her death. Unfortunately, the skull of the skeleton was later lost in Germany during the Second World War.

In classical antiquity, intramural burials were reserved for the most prominent persons, such as heroes, wealthy sponsors of public buildings, or influential politicians. Thus, the archaeologists were more than surprised to discover the mausoleum apparently erected to honour a very young woman. As no inscription was found to explain who it had been, the riddle is still unsolved. However, a sensational suggestion was made in the 80-ties of the 20th century. Hilke Thür of the Austrian Academy of Sciences suggested that it was the tomb of Arsinoë IV, an Egyptian princess murdered in 41 BCE by Mark Antony, at the instigation of Cleopatra VII.

The dating of the tomb seemed to confirm this theory, as it was dated to the period between 50 and 20 BCE. Moreover, the octagonal plan of the monument that resembles the second tier of the Lighthouse of Alexandria and the pyramidal shape of the mausoleum's roof seem to point out in the direction of Egypt. However, the carbon-dating of the bones conducted in that period gave an extensive range of dates, between 200 and 20 BCE.

The author of "the tomb of Arsinoë" theory, Hilke Thür, made many attempts to prove her point. DNA tests failed because the bones had been handled too many times. Thus, a reconstruction of the missing skull was made, based on the old photographs and measurements made in the 1920s. The computer reconstruction supposedly demonstrated a mixture of African, Egyptian, and classical Grecian features — precisely as it should be expected of Arsinoë's appearance. However, the method of reconstructing the ancestry on the basis of skull measurements has long been discarded as a pseudoscience.

The best summary of the "the tomb of Arsinoë" theory was provided by a renown classicist, Mary Beard, who pointed out the reasons why this interpretation does not add up. Firstly, there is no preserved inscription with the Egyptian princess' name on the tomb. Secondly, the remaining bones (minus the missing skull) are said to be of a 15-18-year-old person, while Arsinoë may well have been in her mid-20s when she was killed. Thirdly, the assumption that Cleopatra and Arsinoë were full sisters is not confirmed because the only certain thing is that their father was King Ptolemy, while they may have had different mothers. This case nullifies the ethnic argument and any genetic or measurement trials. It is also essential to add that some researchers moved the construction date of the Octagon to the times of Emperor Augustus (27 BCE — 14 CE).

However, the sensational idea that the Octagon is the tomb of Arsinoë IV is still widely accepted. Even the official information board placed on-site claims, although cautiously, that "the grave was probably Arsinoë IV, the youngest sister of Cleopatra murdered at Ephesus." If the monument is the tomb of Arsinoë, this would be the only case when the remains of the Ptolemaic dynasty member have been recovered. This fact is even more surprising as this dynasty ruled Egypt for almost 300 years.

On a much down-to-earth tone, the Octagon was later reused in the 4th century CE when two letters were made public in the form of the inscriptions. The first (left) one was written in Latin by the emperors Valentinian, Valens, and Gratian. It concerns the regulation of the public funds division between the cities of Asia Minor heavily damaged by earthquakes. The second (right) inscription is bilingual (in Greek and Latin). Written to the proconsul, it is about the sharing of the costs of the provincial festival games among four cities. It would seem that by the 4th century, the Octagon became a kind of information board where public notices were displayed.

Hexagon

Between the Octagon to the west and the Stoa of Alytarches to the east, the excavations conducted in 1994 revealed the remains of a structure erected on a hexagonal plan and thus dubbed "the Hexagon". The building had been hidden under later-period structures and partly — under the steps of Curetes Street. The archaeologists removed some slabs covering the paved street to reveal the ground plan of the Hexagon. To minimize the damage, they chose the less-preserved slabs, situated in the western corner of the monument.

The reconstructed appearance of the Hexagon is of a three-storied structure, consisting of a base, an Ionic colonnade, and a conical roof. The building reached a height of around 10 meters. The structure was dated to the late 1st century BCE based on the ceramic fragments found nearby. Its function remains uncertain, as it may have been an honorary monument holding a statue of a prominent person on its second level. Right next to the Hexagon, scant remains of a Hellenistic-era well house have been found, reminiscent of the Hellenistic fountain next to the theatre.

Terrace Houses

GPS coordinates: 37.938210, 27.341400

This sensational area of Ephesus consists of luxurious residential villas, located on the northern slope of Bülbüldağ Hill, next to Curetes Street and opposite the Temple of Hadrian. So far, two housing complexes — Eastern and Western — have been excavated. These houses offer a glimpse into the lives of affluent Ephesians and as such are a must-see during the visit to this ancient city, even if it is necessary to purchase an extra ticket. These villas also help the visitors to realize that ancient Ephesus consisted not only of public building but also of residential units. Finally, looking at the still unexcavated slopes of Bülbüldağ Hill, one has to wonder how many more of such magnificent dwellings are still hidden below the ground.

As it is also true in modern cities, there were more and less prestigious locations in Ephesus. Curetes Street, centrally located and linking the most important public spaces of the city, was undoubtedly among the highly desired addresses. The prominent location of the Terrace Houses — in the heart of the city — meant that these were the dwellings of wealthy and influential people. These residences are excellent examples of the so-called peristyle houses. As "peri" means around and "style" means a column, so a peristyle is a place with columns around it. The peristyle houses consisted of a courtyard (atrium) open to the sky, with a covered walkway around a garden, and with columns holding up the roof. Rooms, kitchens, working and storage areas were all situated around this courtyard. The Ephesus houses are among the best-preserved ex-

Mosaic floors of the Terraced Houses

amples of such residences, but it is also possible to see similar ones elsewhere, for instance, in Pompeii.

The Terrace Houses in Ephesus were two- or three-storied, with living quarters mainly on the ground floor. The construction materials were carefully selected to keep the houses cool in summer and warm in winter. They were also equipped with running water and central heating system. The luxurious style of living there was also reflected in magnificent mosaics and marble slabs covering the floors, and intricate frescoes on the walls.

However, it had not always been a residential quarter of Ephesus. Until the 4th century BCE, the northern slopes of Bülbüldağ Hill had been used as a cemetery. Only with the relocation of the city by King Lysimachus in the early 3rd century BCE, these slopes were designated for the residential units of Ephesus. The intensification of the construction work of the Terrace Houses took place in the times of Octavian Augustus but was interrupted by an earthquake. The residences were then restored and flourished until another series of disastrous earthquakes — in 355, 358, and 368 CE.

After another reconstruction, in the 5th century CE, the residences were rearranged to suit the needs of the early-Christian period. The houses suffered destruction by the Arab raids at the end of the 6th century CE, and were later rebuilt for the last time, with spolia material from the earlier buildings. However, they lost their original function of prestigious residences and served as a space for many workshops, for instance, as a smithy and a mill complex. The flour mill installation was added gradually over a period of one hundred years, and reached the greatest capacity at the turn of the 6th and the 7th centuries. At that time, the mills running in the former villas could produce enough flour to feed up to twelve thousand people. The buildings were finally abandoned by the end of the 7th century, and some water mills were later erected to the west.

Following the sightseeing tour of the Terrace Houses, the visitors can see the Eastern House, called Terrace House II, first. It occupies an area of about 2500 square meters and consists of private houses, built on three terraces. There were seven residential units in this area, all of them were two stories high, and some had numerous entrances in successive terraces. Due to the long period of their occupancy, these apartments underwent multiple structural changes, and some dwellings were created by dividing a more substantial house into smaller units.

A visitor to one of these apartments entered the ground floor level from the steep alley climbing Bülbüldağ Hill and passed into a vestibule or a more spacious atrium. From this viewpoint, the guest could see the peristyle courtyard, open to the sky, and lavishly decorated with sculptures. In some cases, there was a fountain in the centre of the courtyard, too. Around the yard, there was a series of rooms, and some of them played the role of a reception space if the guest arrived as a client or a business partner. Some of these rooms were even equipped with windows. Other rooms functioned as banqueting spaces for evening receptions and parties, and some of them were equipped with heating systems for the convenience of the guests in winter.

More private areas of these dwellings were reserved for family and closest friends only. Several of the houses were equipped with an exedra — a semicircular recess — or wide opening overlooking a peristyle with a fountain — a welcome retreat in hot weather for the whole family. Other social spaces identified in several dwellings were associated with cultural functions, such as the so-called Socrates Room in House 4, Muses Room in House 2, or Sapho Room in House 3. They probably played the role of private libraries or concert halls.

The most private quarters of the apartment's owner and his family were located on the upper story. Finally, kitchens and restrooms were hidden from the view of the visitors in the far-away corners of the atrium.

Interestingly, in this Terrace House, possibly not all spaces were private houses. Some researchers, such as Jobst and Scherrer, were particularly interested in apartments 6 and 7 of this unit, situated on the lower levels of the complex. The ground plans of these apartments suggested their use for public purposes, possibly guest accommodation. The owner of these apartments was a priest of Dionysus, Flavius Furius Aptus, who was active at the end of the 2nd century CE. He was known as the organizer of the Ephesian games, and quite possibly prepared these spaces as a 'hotel' for the participants or important visitors.

The most impressive part of the Terrace House II complex was initially identified as a spacious domus, i.e. an urban villa inhabited by wealthy patricians. It covered the area of 1400 square meters and faced Curetes Street. It had a reception room, next to a dining room (a triclinium). A staircase took visitors to the upper level with a waiting room. However, no side rooms, latrines, or baths have been identified in the area of this residence. As it is difficult to imagine a house without these amenities, the researchers have reinterpreted its function as a meeting hall of a professional association or a banqueting house of a prominent citizen, used only for the representational purposes.

The Western Complex, known as Terrace House I, consisted of at least five luxury villas with peristyles, i.e. inner courtyards, perfectly preserved to our times. Many of the rooms are still decorated with frescoes and works of art, discovered during archaeological works. Also in this section, all the houses had running water, and the traces of bathrooms equipped with bathtubs have been found.

Nowadays, Terrace House II has been covered under a roof for protection from the elements. Here, the paths for visitors have been prepared to follow the sightseeing tour. Numerous information boards explain the details of the visible structures. Moreover, reconstruction works continue in the villas. This fact allows the visitors to appreciate the painstaking work of archaeologists putting together marble slabs as a kind of a gigantic puzzle. Terrace House I still awaits similar protection and is currently off-limits to the visitors.

Temple of Hadrian

GPS coordinates: 37.938538, 27.341943

A temple-like monument, known as the Temple of Hadrian, stands in front of the Scholastica (Varius) Baths, facing the Curetes Street. When it was discovered in 1956 and subsequently re-erected in the following two years, it was commonly assumed that it really was the Temple of Emperor Hadrian, a "neocorate temple" of official worship of the Roman emperor. The permission to build such a temple in Ephesus was granted by Hadrian between 130 and 132 CE, and the archaeologists eagerly identified the building on Curetes Street as such.

The inscription placed on the architrave blocks of the building informs that it was dedicated to Hadrian and the neokoros demos of Ephesus by P. Quintilius Valens Varius, his wife, and his daughter, under the grammateus Ti. Claudius Lucceianus; it was inaugurated under the proconsul Q. Servaeus Innocens and the twice grammateus and asiarch P. Vedius Antoninus. P. Quintilius Valens Varius is the same person as the sponsor of the baths behind the temple.

However, many researchers today question this identification and point out to the much larger Temple of Hadrian/Olympieion near the Church of Mary instead. There are many reasons for the re-interpretation of this structure, as convincingly discussed by Ursula Quatember. She explains that the erection date of the temple has been pushed back in time to the period of 117-119 CE. The motive for the reassessment of the dates is the presence of two people in the dedicatory inscription: Q. Servaeus Innocens and

Temple of Hadrian rebuilt from original fragments

P. Vedius Antoninus who were active in the earlier period. This would mean that the building had been constructed around 10–15 years before Ephesus received permission to build a neocorate temple for Hadrian.

Almost all researchers are now in agreement that the "true" neocorate Temple of Hadrian is the one found in the so-called Olympieion area. However, several radical theories try to explain the true nature of the so-called Temple of Hadrian on Curetes Street. For instance, it was suggested that the building had been a memorial for Hadrian's lover, Antinous.

Some scholars even discarded the idea that the building was actually a temple. In this view, the structure now decorating Curetes Street had originally been the propylon of the Hadrian's Temple in the Olympieion area, later re-used in the renovation of the Varius Baths. Such rather wild speculations have recently been rejected by Quatember who, after a detailed architectural analysis, has convincingly demonstrated that in its original conception the "Temple of Hadrian" was planned and erected together with the Varius Baths. Moreover, both buildings are tied together by their architecture.

The Temple of Hadrian, despite its small dimensions of 10 to 10 meters in the plan, is one of the most attractive structures in Ephesus. It reaches a height of about 8 meters. This modest-sized building is divided into two spaces: a front hall (pronaos) and a main room (cella). It is described as a variation of the tetrastyle prostyle plan. The prostyle means that it has a row of columns in front, and the tetrastyle specifies that there are four of them. In the case of the Temple of Hadrian, this design was modified, with two pillars on the sides and two regular columns placed between them.

The pillars and columns, standing in front of the pronaos, are in the Corinthian order. They support a pediment with an arch in the centre, decorated with a bust of Tyche surrounded by acanthus leaves. The architrave is beautifully adorned with plant motifs and the dedicatory inscription discussed above. This design was most probably prepared by an architect from Syria, as this style was common there.

The cella of the temple, in contract to the pronaos, was very simply decorated and there was the base of the cult statue against the back wall, aligned with the entrance. It possibly once held the statue of Emperor Hadrian. The cella was 7.5 meters wide and 5 meters long. It was roofed by a barrel vault. The tympanum above the door to the cella was decorated with the relief of Medusa, set among acanthus leaves and scrolls.

The building was later modified, following an earthquake in the 4th century. Four reliefs, placed in the pronaos, are most commonly dated to the end of the 4th century, but other theories state that they date back to the 3rd century, or even to the original structure. The dating of the reliefs has not been satisfactorily explained so far. These reliefs depict the foundation myth of Ephesus, an anonymous emperor sacrificing in front of a garlanded altar, four Amazons fleeing from Dionysus, and a gathering of deities and heroes. The reliefs that can be seen today in Ephesus are the copies, and the originals are displayed in the Ephesus Museum in Selçuk.

Another later addition to the temple were four statues, placed in front of the building. Their pedestals are still in the original location, but the statues have not been found. It is commonly assumed that they depicted the tetrarchs: Diocletian, Maximian, Constantius Chlorus, and Galerius. Later, Emperor Theodosius possibly substituted the one for Maximian with the statue of his father, as part of his refurbishment of Curetes Street.

The building of the so-called Temple of Hadrian was destroyed at an unknown date, and its blocks were reused for the construction of the retaining wall in the middle of Curetes Street. This wall was erected to prevent the debris from devastated structures and abandoned hillside areas from falling onto the street. The monument we can see today was rebuilt from original fragments with the supplementation of modern building materials in 1957-1958. It subsequently underwent an extensive conservation project from 2012 to 2014.

Trajan's Nymphaeum

GPS coordinates: 37.938121, 27.342502

The look at the north-eastern side of the Curetes Street offers us a glimpse into the secrets of water supply to Ephesus, as in this part of the city numerous monuments dedicated to this function were erected. The first one of them, as one walks down the street, is the Trajan's Nymphaeum. The construction of this monument was part of an ambitious project which also included the erection of a massive aqueduct, already mentioned in the chapter devoted to the theatre of Ephesus as the water-supply was conducted along its upper tiers.

However, it was not the first or the only aqueduct that supplied water to Ephesus. The city as large and prosperous as the ancient Ephesus could not function without a reliable water supply. Its residents needed clean drinking water, as well as water for bathing. The famous public baths and latrines also required much water. Where did it come from? The answer is amazing — Ephesus had not one but four long-distance water conveyance systems.

Until the times of Tiberius Claudius Aristion, Ephesus was supplied with water by three aqueducts. The first one was the Aqua Iulia (or Kenchrios), most probably sponsored by Octavian Augustus and later extended when the second conduit was added, possibly after the earthquake of 178 CE. It is now known as Değirmendere, i.e. the Miller's Stream. This impressive system was 36 kilometres long and supplied water from the springs in the south-western hills, near modern-era Kuşadası. The conduit still exists in quite a good condition, and basically, it is a covered masonry canal, partly cut in the rock. It crosses numerous valleys on its way, utilizing over 20 aqueducts, with single or multiple arches. The longest of these aqueducts is Arvalya with an impressive length of 400 meters, and the highest is Sabancık, reaching 20 meters in height. The conveyance system passes through a 335 m long tunnel, just about one kilometre away from Ephesus, and reaches the city northwest of the Bülbüldağ Hill.

The second water conveyance system to Ephesus was erected during the reign of emperors Augustus and Tiberius, under the governorships of Gaius Sextilius Pollio and Gaius Offilius Proculus. The system, called Throessitica and now referred to as Derbentdere or Marnas, is relatively short, with a length of seven kilometres only. It diverted the water of springs southeast of Ephesus through baked clay pipes, with not one but three almost parallel lines. The oldest of these lines dates back to a much earlier period of the 3rd century BCE. It means that Ephesus was one of the few cities supplied by a major water system already in the Hellenistic times. The clay pipes of the system once carried 20 litres of water per second. The Derbentdere water conveyance system follows the northeastern hill-slopes of Bülbüldağ Hill, crosses two narrow valleys over single-arched aqueducts and reaches Ephesus to the south of the Magnesia Gate.

The most impressive element of this system is the Sextilius Pollio aqueduct, dating back to the early years of the 1st century CE. According to inscriptions on either side of the aqueduct, a certain Sextilius Pollio, along with his wife and stepson, provided funds for its construction, hence the aqueduct's name. It is 16 meters high, has three arches of more than 5-metre span at the lower level and six arches with the span of 2.75 meters at the higher level. The aqueduct stands near the road from Selçuk to Çamlık, around 1.5 kilometres to the south of Acarlar village.

The third water conveyance system to Ephesus was called the Selenus, and today is referred to as the Şirince Aqueduct. It was eight kilometres long and also consisted of baked clay pipes that transported 10 litres of water per second. It was fed by ground-

Trajan's Nymphaeum seen from Curetes Street

water near the village of Şirince to the east of Ephesus. The lead pipes with marble joints discovered under the floor of the Artemis Temple's altar were probably the final part of this conveyance system. It means that the original system may date back to the 6th century BCE. However, later it underwent several repairs and extensions, for instance in the 6th century CE. It was then extended to carry water to the Ayasuluk Hill and Saint John Basilica when the 650-meters-long aqueduct was built, still visible in the modern town of Selçuk. Even in the 14th century, the system was still in use, when the Turks extended it again, to provide water to İsa Bey Mosque and its baths.

Thus, by the time of Tiberius Claudius Aristion, Ephesus already had three water conveyance systems. However, the fourth system, sponsored by Aristion in 114 CE, was the longest of them, as it covered the distance of 42 kilometres. It brought water to the city from Kayapınar (ancient Kaystros River) springs close to the village of Kurşak near Belevi, to the northeast of Ephesus. The system is known as Claudius Aristion, Kayapınar, or Kaystros. This system was built as a masonry conduit and carried between 100 and 200 litres of water per second.

After crossing many valleys over single-arched aqueducts, the conduit reached the vicinity of Ephesus, following the contour lines of the slopes of the Pion (Panayır Dağ) Hill, passing near the Grotto of Seven Sleepers. It reached the city at the stadium, where it was conducted as a masonry gallery under the seats. Next, it passed under the central seat rows of the theatre's upper tier and discharged into the Trajan's Nymphaeum. Passing under the Curetes Street, the system also supplied water to the Terrace Houses on the slope of Bülbüldağ Hill.

The Trajan's Nymphaeum has the shape of a pool surrounded on three sides by a two-storey structure. Like Rome, ancient Ephesus was also a city of fountains. Nowadays, with the running water readily available in our kitchens and bathrooms, we frequently underestimate the function of public fountains, treating them as a purely decorative element of the cityscape.

However, in ancient cities of the Roman era, the majority of households had to draw drinking water from such fountains, and every day citizens, servants, and slaves rushed with vessels and buckets to fill them at the public fountains. These structures varied from simple ones to the elaborate monuments paid for by wealthy sponsors to commemorate their names or pay respects to the rulers of the Empire.

Trajan's Nymphaeum definitely belongs to the second category. This monumental building was erected in honour of Artemis of Ephesus and Emperor Trajan by Tiberius Claudius Aristion and his wife, as an inscription informs us: "Claudius Aristion, thrice asiarch and neokoros, with his wife Julia Lydia Laterane [...] daughter of Asia, high-priestess and prytanis, he dedicated the [...] water, having brought it 210 stadia through the water conduit he constructed, and the water reservoir, with all its decorations, at his own expense, to Ephesian Artemis and to the Emperor Nerva Trajan Caesar Augustus Germanicus Dacicus and to the fatherland."

To fully realize the massive dimensions of the Trajan's Nymphaeum, it is necessary to visualize Curetes Street in its heyday, when it was a colonnaded thoroughfare, with two parallel rows of columns running from its beginning to the end. The nymphaeum, around 9.5 meters high and 17 meters long, slightly jutting outwards, dwarfed all the surrounding area.

At least ten statues were located in the various niches of the fountain. During the archaeological excavations of the nymphaeum, the researchers found the statue of Aphrodite, two statues of Dionysos, naked and clothed, a young hunter symbolizing the founder of the city, Androklos, Emperor Nerva, some women, and one satyr in a lying position. All of these findings are exhibited in the Ephesus Museum in Selçuk.

The most important decoration of the fountain was the colossal statue of Emperor Trajan, twice the size of the other statues, standing in the centre of the building, from which the water flowed into the pool. The emperor was depicted with a globe under his feet, in a nude heroic posture according to the Greek tradition.

Unfortunately, only the base of the statue and imperial feet have been preserved.

The fountain was ornamented with the Corinthian and composite columns. It had not one but two ornamental pools, one in the front and one at the rear, with two tiers of columns. The pipes filled the pools with water. When the back pool was full, the water flew via a channel into the front pool.

Who was the sponsor of this impressive monument? Tiberius Claudius Aristion, a prominent citizen of Ephesus, started his political career as grammateus — the secretary of the people. Then, he held the offices of prytanis, the president of the city council of Ephesus, and gymnasiarchos, the magistrate who was responsible for the gymnastic and literary instruction. As such, he sponsored the provision of oil for the city's main gymnasium. Finally, he reached the positions of archiereus, the high priest of the imperial cult, and neokoros, the guardian of the imperial temple. It is quite possible that he was personally responsible for the erection of the Temple of Domitian, later converted into the Temple of the Sebastoi.

Ariston's popularity and wealth brought him the jealousy of some people as attested by Pliny the Younger, who explains that: "Claudius Aristo, the leading citizen at Ephesus, a man of great generosity, and who had won popularity by innocent means, pleaded his own case. His popularity had made people envious of him, and some of his enemies, who were utterly unlike him in character, had suborned a man to lay information against him. So he was acquitted, and his reputation vindicated." When Ariston died, he was buried within the city walls, as was the common practice with the most influential citizens of Ephesus. His sarcophagus was later moved to the vicinity of the Androklos Heroon.

Alytarches' Stoa

GPS coordinates: 37.937526, 27.342903

The south-western section of Curetes Street in Ephesus finished with the so-called Alytarches' Stoa, to the east of the Hellenistic Fountain. It was a 53-meter-long structure, 4 to 5 meters wide, and divided into two sections because of the variance in the ground level.

The stoa hid a row of twelve shops and workshops, and a narrow alley leading up Bülbüldağ Hill. This street was adapted to the steep slope of the hill, with flights of steps overcoming the level differences. It led to the residential units arranged in pairs on terraces, currently known as the Terrace Houses. The alley only reached the Alytarches' Stoa that played the role of a foyer for these houses.

The stoa's floor was covered at its full length with mosaics, composed of geometric patterns, with the addition of flowers and birds. This mosaic, comprised of many sections, covered an impressive area of 285 square meters.

The original design of the Alytarches' Stoa is unclear, but we can safely presume that its excavated version of late antiquity was a project of reconstruction. It is challenging to imagine that there had been no colonnades or shops along this stretch of Curetes Street earlier on.

The Alytarches' Stoa was renovated in the early 5th century CE by a city official bearing the title of Alytarches — responsible for the observance of rules during athletic contests. The restoration must have been finished by 440 CE, as a letter to the proconsul of

Alytarches' Stoa with visible mosaic floor

this year, Flavius Heliodorus, was carved on one of its columns.

As the title of Alytarches has been mentioned, we can use this opportunity to have a closer look at the sports events held in ancient Ephesus. The athletic contests in Ephesus were usually held at the city's stadium, located to the north-east of Ephesus, just to the south of the Vedius Gymnasium, in a depression near the Pion Hill. This was the place where celebrations of all kinds were held, including sports events, chariot races, and gladiatorial combats.

Most probably, the first stadium in that location was erected in the Hellenistic times by king Lysimachus in the 3rd century BCE. To create the stadium, an artificial cavity was dug into the ground, covering the area of 3.3 hectares. The surviving traces, the dimensions, and the elongated form of the structure allowed its early identification as a stadium, oriented along the east-west axis. This Hellenistic structure was rather simple with just a flat running track and earthen banks where the spectators could sit, situated on the southern side. It was then used for religious ceremonies and sports activities.

The stadium was subsequently enlarged and rebuilt during the reign of Emperor Nero (54-68 CE) as testified by the discovered inscription. According to this inscription, engraved on the southern retaining wall of the stadium, the refurbishment was funded by a wealthy citizen named C. Stertinius Orpex, his wife Stertinia Marena, and their daughter. The works also covered the construction of vaulted substructures for the marble seats on the north side.

It is possible that the first gladiatorial games in Asia Minor took place in the stadium of Ephesus. They were organized by Lucius Licinius Lucullus who arrived in Asia Minor to participate in the Third Mithridatic War. Plutarch described his stay in Ephesus in the biography of Lucullus in the famous series of Parallel Lives: "Lucullus, after filling Asia full of law and order, and full of peace, did not neglect the things which minister to pleasure and win favour, but during his stay at Ephesus gratified the cities with processions and triumphal festivals and contests of athletes and gladiators. And the cities, in response, celebrated festivals which they called Lucullea, to do honour to the man, and bestowed upon him what is sweeter than honour, their genuine good-will."

The stadium was a U-shaped building measuring 229 by 28 meters. The seats for spectators on the southern side were built into the slope of Pion Hill (now Panayırdağ). Spectators entered the northern side of the stadium through two outer staircases and a vaulted internal corridor, 85 meters long. In the south-western section of the stadium, there was a monumental gate, still preserved in good condition. Archaeological research has discovered water pipes running through the southern section of the stadium. Quite possibly, they supplied water for mock-naval battles, fashionable during the Roman period.

Sadly, the stadium is not open to the public and has not been restored. The monument was found in 1911, but systematic archaeological research of the site began only in 1993.

Hydreion and Memmius Monument

GPS coordinates: 37.937251, 27.343330

Two important structures adorn the southeastern section of the Curetes Street. They are the Hydreion and the Memmius Monument.

Hydreion

The remains of the impressive fountain known as the Hydreion occupy a space near the intersection of the Curetes Street and the so-called Terrace House Street. This street covered the upper storeys of the Terrace Houses, and it got down and reached the main artery of Curetes Street just at the fountain.

Two water basins have been preserved of the Hydreion, flanked by a semi-circular niche that was originally adorned with many statues. The building inscription informs us that T. Flavius Meander was its founder, during the Severan period, i.e. around 200 CE. However, the reused architectural fragments suggest that there had been an earlier monument in the same location, dating back to the early Imperial period, possibly to the times of Octavian Augustus.

The monument was modified in the late antiquity when the statues of the Tetrarchs — Diocletian, Maximian, Galerius, and Constantius Chlorus — were installed in front of the fountain, similarly as was the case in the so-called Temple of Hadrian. Four Corinthian columns that supported these statues have been re-erected. There are also indications that the fountain itself was repaired in the 4th century CE.

It is believed that the Hydreion served more than just a deco-

Hydreion and Memmius Monument

rative purpose. With a large amount of traffic along the Curetes Street, the water was used to keep the street clean and to keep the marble surface wet during the hot summer months. The area at the Memmius Monument and the Hydreion also created a small square where the people walking along the Curetes Street could rest for a while in the shade. One can imagine the weary travellers sitting there, gazing up the Curetes Street and listening to the sound of flowing water.

Memmius Monument

The monument behind the Hydreion, on the other hand, served a more dignified purpose by reminding the citizens of Ephesus of some grim events from the city's past. The Memmius Monument was a memorial built during the reign of Octavian Augustus.

The inscription of the monument referred to Lucius Cornelius Sulla's capture of the city after the Mithridatic Wars in the 1st century BCE. The inscription also informs that the statue of Lucius Cornelius Sulla once stood on the base built of stone blocks.

The founder of the monument, Gaius Memmius, was the son of Gaius Memmius and Fausta Cornelia, the daughter of Lucius Cornelius Sulla. Thus, he was a grandson of Sulla, the former dictator of Rome. However, very little is known of Gaius Memmius' career. He served as consul suffectus in 34 BCE and was later appointed to the position of a proconsular governor of Asia, sometime after 30 BCE.

He erected the so-called Memmius Monument to honour himself and three generations of his family. The inscription reads "To Gaius Memmius, son of Gaius Memmius, grandson of Sulla Felix (paid for this monument) from his own funds."

The monument originally had a form of a four-sided victory arch, and there were three sets of stairs between the columns holding an arch. The memorial had four facades depicting Sulla's army and the reliefs symbolizing the virtues of the dictator. Sulla, his son Gaius Memmius, and his grandson (also Gaius Memmius) are depicted on the reliefs of this monument of ancestral glory.

Domitian Square

GPS coordinates: 37.936787, 27.343329

Domitian Square, located at the southeastern end of the Curetes Street, is dominated by the Temple of the Imperial Cult and its artificial terrace. This enormous square is bordered from the east by a series of buildings along the so-called Domitian Street. These buildings — the Chalcidium, the Pollio Monument, and the Fountain of Domitian — also demarcate the western side of the State Agora.

The characteristic round base decorated with garlands carried by bulls' heads stands in the centre of the Domitian Square. It was moved into this location from some other part of the city, possibly in the middle of the 4th century. This could be a sacrificial altar, and its decorations symbolize fertility and abundance.

Flanked by taverns and shops, the Domitian Street climbed in the southern direction, following the eastern side of the Temple of the Imperial Cult's substructure. It is not certain if this substructure, the so-called cryptoporticus, was accessible to passers-by. However, its well-lit and ventilated corridors would have provided ideal space for storage. Quite recently, these rooms were used by the archaeologists to house the Inscription Museum, but it is now permanently closed.

Chalcidium

The first structure among this rather crowded for the eye assembly of buildings along Domitian Street, walking from the north, is the Chalcidium. This projecting bulk of massive ashlar blocks is hard

Round base with garlands carried by bulls' heads in the centre of Domitian Square

to miss. Its name means a portico or a hall that formed an annexe to an ancient Roman basilica.

In Ephesus, it played the function of a substructure supporting the western end of the Basilica Stoa of the State Agora, and it was probably added in the times of Emperor Nero. The three chambers of the Chalcidium projected out to the Domitian Square through the doorways opening directly to the square.

Pollio Monument

Just next to the Chalcidium stands the structure known as the Pollio Monument. It was erected in the form of a memorial tomb by the stepson of Gaius Sextilius Pollio in the area designated to honour his valuable donations to Ephesus. For instance, Pollio sponsored the water conveyance system that brought water to Ephesus via the Pollio Aqueduct. Moreover, he also paid for the Basilica Stoa of the State Agora. The dimensions of the Pollio Monument are 8 to 6.5 meters, and its current height is 6.4 meters.

The Pollio Monument was later expanded when the large semi-domed apsidal construction of the Fountain of Domitian was added to its southern part in 92/93 CE. Water brought by the aqueducts to the city was distributed from this fountain by a branching system of baked clay pipes. The structure has been recently restored with the final effect clearly visible as the previously used grey concrete fillings are now replaced with the ones that blend in more with the original elements.

The most exciting find from this fountain was a group of statues that adorned it. These statues were not made especially for this monument, but they were brought here from other locations. The most spectacular of them is the group representing the familiar theme of the blinding of the Cyclops by Odysseus and his companions, frequently referred to as the Polyphemus Group. The group dates back to the 1st century BCE. Other sculptures represent the river gods — Marnas and Klaseas — that had been placed in the northern and southern niches, while the statue of Zeus stood in the central, western niche. The Polyphemus Group and other statues are now on display in the Ephesus Museum in Selçuk.

Temple of the Imperial Cult

Finally, let us have a closer look at the so-called Temple of Domitian that dominated this quarter of the city, on the western side of the State Agora. According to the theory that was widely accepted in the past, this enormous temple of the Imperial Cult was supposedly erected to honour Emperor Domitian, the second son of Emperor Vespasian. The temple building stood on the slopes of Bülbüldağı Hill, on an artificially created terrace.

Because the area that is now covered by the Domitian Square had been originally a valley between the hills, a massive vaulted substructure was necessary to carry the weight of the temple. This rectangular terrace measured 50 to 100 meters, and it reached the height of the State Agora.

The Ephesians erected this temple at an enormous expense, in the best and most central part of their city, opposite the State Agora. Moreover, it was the first temple in Ephesus built in honour of a Roman emperor, as Domitian was the first of the emperors who gave permission to built such a temple. Thus, during his reign, Ephesus became the neokoros, i.e. temple-warden, for the first time, which was a great honour for a city.

The ground plan of the temple was reconstructed based on the excavations carried out in the 1930s. The reconstruction of the superstructure of the temple has not been possible, as only a few fragments of the building itself have been found. On the other hand, the temple appears on several coins minted in Ephesus. The temple was a typical Roman prostyle-type structure, which means that four columns stood in front of its vestibule. It was also surrounded by a single colonnade, with 13 columns along its longer sides, and eight columns on the shorter sides.

The main chamber of the temple — its cella — was small, as it measured only 9 to 17 meters. Its stylobate, the top step of the stepped platform, upon which colonnades were placed, had the dimensions of 24 to 34 meters. Eight steps led up from the street level to the top of this platform. The main entrance was located in the north, and, in addition, a secondary entry was identified in the west.

The temple had one unusual feature: when the visitors ascended the stairs to the top of the platform, they did not immediately see the temple itself. Instead, they were greeted by a U-shaped altar, standing 10 metres in front of the temple. This solution, not known in other parts of the Roman Empire, was similar to the plan of the Artemision but also several other major temples in Asia Minor, such as the Artemis Temple in Sardis, the Athena Temple in Priene, and the Artemis Leukophryene Temple in Magnesia on the Meander.

The altar, decorated with a relief frieze depicting scenes of sacrifice and representations of weapons, is now on display in the Ephesus Museum in Selçuk along with the fragments of a monumental statue that was once identified as the one depicting Emperor Domitian. Nowadays, the scholars tend to agree that it was a statue of Domitian's older brother, Titus.

After Emperor Domitian was murdered and the Roman senate condemned him to damnatio memoriae (condemnation of memory), the Ephesians had to rename the magnificent temple erected in his honour. It must have been an awkward situation for the Ephesians, who had received many favours from this emperor. Not only had he provided tax breaks for the Temple of Artemis by extending its boundaries, but also supported the construction of a new water supply system. The revenues from the Artemision may have been used to sponsor the re-pavement of Curetes Street and the renovation of the theatre.

However, the Ephesians had to follow the instructions from Rome. Their solution was very simple as they just rededicated the temple to Domitian's father, Emperor Vespasian, and his brother, Emperor Titus. Thus, later the building was often referred to as the Temple of the Emperors or, in the Greek form, the Temple of Sebastoi. Actually, from that moment on, the Ephesians started frequently using the term theoi sebastoi, meaning the divine Augusti, possibly to avoid future alterations of the temple's inscriptions.

The temple was discovered in 1930 by J. Keil who was searching for the location of the Parthian Monument. The excavations conducted in that period revealed the cella of the temple and some sections of the stepped substructure. Moreover, a test trench was dug over the courtyard, revealing the existence of an altar there. The ground plan of the temple, created then by M. Theuer is still accepted as correct.

The identification of the building as the Temple of Domitian was based on the discovery of two fragments of the colossal statue, discovered as the elements of the Byzantine wall erected into the substructure. Based on these findings, connected with the numismatic and epigraphic material, Keil deducted that this was indeed an imperial cult sanctuary.

Only in 1958, further work was conducted in the area of the temple, continuing until 1962. The excavations, led by F. Miltner and F. Eichler, uncovered a half of the area to the north of the temple. The investigations were also focussed on the so-called Domitian Street, running to the south along the substructure, and the adjacent tabernae (shops and stalls). Establishing that the area had been used earlier, in the Hellenistic period, was the most important result of this phase of works. Moreover, one more fragment of the monumental statue was found — a big toe of the left foot.

From 1969 to 1970, the authorities of the Ephesus Museum in Selçuk organized the removal of the debris from the western side of the cryptoporticus and discovered more fragments of statues. They also concluded that these fragments were not of one but several sculptures. In the 1970s, the architectural history of the area was studied.

The excavations of 2009 and 2011 resulted in the dating of the temple's destruction to the early 5th century CE. The temple was demolished systematically and purposefully, and the inscriptions were carefully erased before the stone blocks could be reused. While the temple was demolished down to its substructure, another building was erected on its place in the early Byzantine period.

It had massive walls and the floor raised by 1.5 meters. Its solid construction suggests that it was an element of the fortifications, situated in a strategic location between the Byzantine settlement in the former Lower City and the hinterland.

The yard to the east of the temple was also used in the Byzantine period. The excavations have been conducted in this area since 2011. So far, they have revealed an impressive building complex with a marble-paved courtyard, a room with a polychrome mosaic floor depicting marine creatures, a fountain, and commercial spaces. These rooms testify to the high standard of living in the period between the 5th and the 6th centuries CE.

State Agora

GPS coordinates: 37.936363, 27.344286

The spacious area situated on the plateau between Pion (Panayır Dağ) and Koressos (Bülbül Dağ) Hills is known as the Upper City of Ephesus. In this location, the archaeologists identified an extensive residential quarter of the city, covering around 50 hectares. The area was settled during the Hellenistic-period urbanization. It was organized according to the traditional grid-plan, known from Miletus. In the case of Ephesus, the grid system of the Upper City was drawn with the South Street, the one leading to the Magnesia Gate, as the baseline, and the Domitian Street as the western border. This quarter was divided by 24 streets oriented from the north to the south, and seven streets from the east to the west. This dense grid of the streets complied with the topography of the ground, and the land available for the building was used as efficiently as it was possible.

The grid created 88 construction parcels (i.e. the insulae) in total, with individual houses covering a part of one block and larger peristyle-houses — a whole block. The discovered drainage systems and water conduits provided evidence of the excellent infrastructure of the quarter. Its street grid plan remained almost unchanged from the Hellenistic period well into the late antiquity. The large part of the Upper City of Ephesus, situated to the south-east, is still awaiting the excavations and is not open for the tourists.

The north-western part of the Upper Town is covered by the State (Upper) Agora that occupies four building parcels. In every significant ancient settlement founded by the Greeks, the main

State Agora seen from the south with Pion Hill in the background

square called the agora played the central role in the life of the city. Ephesus had two agoras — a political one and a commercial one — situated at opposite ends of the city. The spacious State Agora was located in the south-eastern part of Ephesus, while the Commercial Agora — in the north-western part of the city.

The original plan of the State Agora dates back to the 4th century BCE, when it was created in the area of an older cemetery. It has been confirmed by archaeological excavations carried out in its north-eastern corner. Numerous graves from the 7th and the 6th centuries BCE were found there, along with an archaic sarcophagus of terracotta. Thus, as it is also the case of the Lower Agora, this square was created in the location of an old necropolis — this fact demonstrates how quickly the city had expanded beyond the previously planned boundaries.

The Upper Agora received its urban character between the Hellenistic and the early Roman period. The square was paved around 65 BCE by Timon, the agoranomos, i.e. the market overseer. Finally, it was renovated at the beginning of the 1st century CE.

The Public Agora served as a place for official and public meetings. It has dimensions of 160 by 73 meters, and was once surrounded on three sides by colonnades. The western side was bordered by an ashlar wall, against which several monuments were erected on the eastern side of the Domitian Square. The stoas served as roofed walkways, lavishly decorated with sculptures, and provided shelter from rain and heat. These stoas were not only ideal for the citizens who wished to discuss politics, but also played the role of classrooms where teachers and philosophers could gather their students.

STOA BASILICA

The northern colonnade is often referred to as the Stoa Basilica due to its impressive design. This two-storied structure had two aisles and a central nave, divided by two rows of columns in Ionic order decorated with bulls' heads on two sides. There is a reason for this peculiar design: the heads lengthen the support for the architrave, making it possible to place the columns holding up the roof of the stoa over five meters apart. Moreover, the bulls' heads emphasized the hall's sacred aura, documenting that the basilica also served as a place of worship.

In total, there were 67 such columns, situated along the basilica that was 168 meters long and 16 meters wide. The entrances were through the long side facing the agora. The stoa was erected in 11 CE and later modified. The sponsor of the stoa was again C. Sextilius Pollio who dedicated it to Artemis, Augustus, and Tiberius. The dedicatory inscription was written both in Greek and in Latin. This impressive basilica replaced an earlier, Hellenistic single-aisled stoa, situated 1.3 meters below, as confirmed by the excavations.

The statues of Emperor Augustus and his wife Livia stood at the eastern entrance to the basilica, in the special room used as the ceremonial hall. The hall was demolished in the early Byzantine period, and the statues were 'Christianized' by carving crosses on their foreheads. Now, these statues can be seen in the Ephesus Museum in Selçuk.

The Chalcidium (a vestibule), discussed in the chapter devoted to Domitian Square, was added to its western side during the reign of Emperor Nero. Finally, in the late Roman Imperial period, additional columns with Corinthian capitals were added between the original Ionic ones, to offer extra support. The Stoa Basilica was, most probably, the place of municipal activities, such as court proceedings or public meetings, due to its proximity to the Prytaneion.

Southern Stoa

While most of the visitors only stroll along the northern side of the State Agora, it is also possible to walk along its southern edge, where the traces of the Southern Stoa and the Magnesia Road can be seen. Moreover, this part of the ancient city is an oasis of peace and quiet, even on the busiest days.

The construction of the Southern Stoa took place in the first half of the 2nd century BCE, but by the late 6th century CE at the latest, the stoa was destroyed. When it still existed, it was a two-story hall, around 160 meters long. Later, it was shortened when a small gate building was added in the south-eastern part of the Upper Agora. Possibly at the same time, the Upper Agora also received a monumental new entrance, located in the middle of the back wall of the hall.

The southern side of the State Agora was separated from the road to the Magnesian Gate by a colonnade facing a solid wall. In the south-eastern corner of the agora, there was a large cistern for the water brought by the Marnas supply system. The water was later distributed throughout the city through the terracotta pipes, discovered under the agora. The south-western corner of the agora was occupied by a magnificent fountain of Laecanius Bassus.

Along the Magnesian Road, running parallel to the southern stoa, approximately halfway between the corners of the State Agora, stood another monumental fountain of the city. The road is still there, paved with slabs and lined with columns. The lower part of the fountain was erected of stones and the upper part — of bricks. A hemispherical niche is still visible in the back of the structure. The front of the nymphaeum, visible from the Magnesian Road, is semicircular in plan and built of ashlar stones. The vantage point next to this ruined fountain offers excellent views of the State Agora, the Bouleuterion, and the Prytaneion, with the Pion Hill in the background.

So-called Temple of Isis

One of the main buildings on the State Agora was an impressive temple, dating back to the 1st century BCE. It stood to the west from the centre of the square. It is commonly called the Temple of Isis, but the more careful archaeologists just describe it as the Temple on the State Agora. That is because, as it is also the case of the so-called Serapis Temple of Ephesus, the exact nature of the deity worshipped here has not been clearly identified.

The temple was excavated in 1970 when its original plan was revealed. It was built on the podium measuring 23 to 15 meters, surrounded by Ionic columns, ten on longer sides and six — on shorter sides. Its façade was adorned with a group of statues depicting the meeting of Odysseus with Polyphemus. This is the same decoration that was later removed and placed in the area of the Pollio Nymphaeum. The dating of the temple itself was based on the dating of these statues that represent the style of the 1st century BCE.

The identification of the temple with the cult of the Egyptian goddess Isis was reached because of the artefacts discovered within its area. These objects include a statue of Ammon, bells symbolizing Isis, and a marble portrait of Mark Antony, known for his pro-Egyptian tendencies.

However, the most recent belief is that the temple was erected later, during the reign of emperors Augustus or Tiberius, around 10-15 CE. This new interpretation, presented on the information board on-site, claims that the temple was a sanctuary of the Association of the Roman Citizens (Conventus Civium Romanorum). It was erected in honour of Divus Caesar and Dea Roma or of Augustus. The building was torn down on the orders of the Emperor Theodosius in the 4th century in the course of alterations which were made in the State Agora.

Public buildings to the north of the State Agora

GPS coordinates: 37.937063, 27.344229

A narrow street, in the ancient times known as Kathodos (The Way Downwards), led from the Domitian Square in the eastern direction, along the northern side of the State Agora. This street offered direct access to the most important religious and civic institutions of Ephesus. On both sides of the street, there are reliefs: one showing Hermes, and one depicting Apollo's tripod. Kathodos Street was hidden from the view of the people on the State Agora.

One can even imagine that it was an official route for the members of Ephesus' governing body, because of the buildings lined up along this street. Walking from the direction of the Domitian Square, the first one was the Banqueting House and the Prytaneion, next was the sacred district of the double-cella temple, and finally — the Bouleuterion.

The so-called Banqueting House was a richly decorated hall 14 to 11 meters large. Its function remains uncertain, as it could have been a place for banquets or a residential house. Most probably, it was functionally related to the Prytaneion.

Prytaneion

In ancient cities of Greek origins, the Prytaneion was the religious and political centre of the community. Each city and town had its own sacred fire of Hestia, the goddess of the hearth, burning within this space, symbolizing the unity and vitality of the people living there. This fire had to be kept burning all the time, tended by the specially designated person. When the city sent the settlers to set up a new colony, they took with them the fire from the altar, to kindle the fire in the newly founded town.

The Prytaneion was not only the central place of the religious cult but also the political heart of the city. It was the location where the prytan held his office. The position of the prytan was of a dual nature: religious and political. Firstly, the prytan was a priest or priestess who ministered in the Prytaneion, the home of Hestia Boulaia (Hestia of the Council) with the sacred fire of the city. Secondly, the prytan was the head of the executive council, chosen from the elite families of the community. In this second role, the prytan's position was similar to the mayor of a city.

The prytan not only had to be from an influential family but also from a wealthy one, as among his responsibilities were the payments of certain expenditures for the city, such as the organization of religious ceremonies. The role of the prytan was not reserved for men only, at least in Asia Minor, where twenty-eight women are known from inscriptions to have held the position. In Ephesus, it is possible to point out two such influential women: Claudia Trophime and Favonia Flacilla.

The writings of Claudia Trophime are one of the rare cases when the work of women writers has survived from antiquity. Claudia Trophime was not only the prytan, but also a priestess of Hera and Hestia. She left two poems praising the goddess for tending the eternal flame, written around 100 CE, These writings were later found in the ruins of Ephesus: "she [the goddess] both gave satisfaction to the gods in their feasts, and tends the blooming fire of our country. Sweetest divinity, flower of the universe, you tend the eternal flame of fire from heaven on your altars."

Favonia Flacilla is known from an inscription dating back to the early 3rd century CE. She offers her gratitude to multiple deities whom she had served and celebrated all the mysteries for a year. The inscription is signed by "prytanis and gymnasiarch, the high-priestess Favonia Flacilla". The second title informs us that her responsibilities were not only of religious nature but also involved

Prytaneion's re-erected columns

the organization of public feasts, festivals, and games.

The Prytaneion of Ephesus, situated just next to the State Agora, was the seat of the rulers of the city where official celebrations, receptions, and banquets were held. The prytan of Ephesus also held the title of the asiarch, i.e. an official who led the provincial assembly and presided over the public games.

However, in the case of Ephesus, the task of tending to the sacred fire belonged not to the prytan, but to the Curetes, the priests affiliated with the Temple of Artemis. Their names are inscribed on the columns of the Prytaneion.

In mythology, the Curetes were known as semi-deities who helped Leto to give birth to Artemis in the grove of Ortygia. According to mythology, while Leto, impregnated by Zeus, was giving birth to the twins, Artemis and Apollo, Curetes made a lot of noise with their weapons. Thanks to that, Zeus's wife Hera, who was jealous of Leto, became confused and did not see the birth of the twins.

The title of 'Curetes' was then given to the priests of the city's protective deity, Artemis. They are mentioned, for instance, by Strabo who explains that: "A general festival is held there annually; and by a certain custom the youths vie for honour, particularly in the splendour of their banquets there. At that time, also, a special college [archeion] of the Curetes holds symposiums and performs certain mystic sacrifices". Unfortunately, the precise nature of the mystical sacrifices remains unknown. Most probably, the aim of the Curetes was to recreate the birth of Artemis Ephesia in Ortygia.

The Curetes were chosen every year, and at first, there were six of them, but later their number was increased to nine. Many inscriptions about the Curetes were discovered in different locations in Ephesus, especially at the Prytaneion. These lists start with the names of the prytan, then enumerates the Curetes, and finally offers the names of numerous cult attendants (hierourgoi). Initially, the Curetes were affiliated only with the Artemision, but during the Roman Empire times, they also acquired a place in the Prytaneion.

The preserved fragments of the Prytaneion are dated to the reign of Emperor Augustus. However, it is believed that there had been an official building in the same location since the Hellenistic period because moving the altar of the eternal flame would be a challenging task.

The Prytaneion was entered through a courtyard surrounded by columns. It also had a façade of six thick columns of the Doric order, and some of them have been re-erected. There were also double columns in the corners of the main hall, while the sacred hearth stood in the centre. The square-shaped area of darker stones in the hall indicated the place of the hearth. The use of columns in the composite order, i.e. combining the elements of Ionic and Corinthian orders, indicates the reconstruction of the Prytaneion in the 3rd century CE.

The building was demolished at the time when the Scholastica Baths were repaired, i.e. around 400 CE, probably as the remainder of the pagan cults. The most interesting objects from the Ephesian Prytaneion are two statues of Artemis of Ephesus that once adorned it. They are currently exhibited in the Ephesus Museum in Selçuk. These famous statues are Roman copies of earlier Greek originals. They were found buried in the Prytaneion. Their preservation, while the Prytaneion itself was destroyed, is sometimes explained by the fact that the cult of Artemis was so firmly embedded that the destroyers of the Prytaneion did not dare touch the statues of the goddess.

Between the Prytaneion and the Bouleuterion, there was the sacred district, enclosed on three sides. Its plan corresponds to the type known as the 'Rhodian Peristyle' with the elevated columnar architecture on the eastern side. On the western side, there was an altar and two smaller temples, erected on a raised podium. The sacred quarter, dating back to the reign of Augustus, was dedicated to the deified Julius Caesar and Goddess Roma or deified Augustus and Artemis. A portrait head of Augustus was found nearby, along with an inscription that mentions the dedication of a statue for Augustus.

The presence of the Temple of the Imperial Cult in the political centre of Ephesus demonstrates the official acknowledgement of the imperial presence and its cult. The double temple with two cellas was an ingenious solution that helped combine two cults within one space. As the temple was erected in the late first century BCE, with the architecture of typical Italian temple design, the sacred building may have been constructed especially for the Romans living in Ephesus.

Bouleuterion

Although the building to the east of the Prytaneion looks like a small theatre, it was the Bouleuterion, the place where the city council met. It was built around 150 CE by Publius Vedius Antoninus. There are canals that provided water drainage in the orchestra, and the entire structure was most likely covered with a roof, to keep the councillors comfortable.

The name bouleuterion comes from the Greek word boule, meaning the group of people appointed to run the daily affairs of the city. Only the most prominent Ephesians had the privilege to participate in these discussions and decide about various aspects of the city's functioning. The city council met at the bouleuterion and received official delegations from other cities and states, under the watchful patronage of Hestia Boulaia, whose sacred flame was burning next door. There were seats that could accommodate around 1400 people inside, so possibly it was simultaneously used as an odeon, i.e. the place of artistic performances.

Baths at the State Agora

The last significant building situated along the northern side of the agora belongs to the so-called Baths at the State Agora. The building is located at the north-eastern corner of the agora, as a continuation of the Stoa Basilica. It is believed that the Roman bathing facility that can still be seen today was erected on the site of an earlier gymnasium from the Hellenistic period. As the land was hilly on the northern side, four bathing rooms of the complex were hewn out of the bedrock to a depth of 6–7 meters.

The caldarium (hot room), at the west, was equipped with seven niches furnished with bathing pools. The colonnades to the south and west, paved with mosaic floors, served as a lobby and recreation rooms. An exercise yard (a palaestra) for sports training and mental development, presumably lies in an unexcavated area to the south. Clay water pipes that supplied water to these baths from the main reservoirs of the city are still visible along the eastern edge of the State Agora.

The end of the tour of Ephesus – or maybe not?

The visit to the Public Agora and the main buildings on its northern side concludes the guided tour of the ancient city of Ephesus. Our aim has been to show you its highlights – the places and structures that are essential to gaining some insights about the functioning of this once great metropolis. However, there is much more to see there – many structures are located off the main visitor path and some of them are currently underground, protected against the elements for the future generations of researchers and tourists. Moreover, some clearly visible structures are closed off to visitors – due to maintenance works and for other reasons. Finally, there are some less popular places in Ephesus open to travellers but still rarely visited, such as a lovely path leading along the southern side of the Public Agora.

Therefore, if you find out after your visit to Ephesus that you are eager to learn more about its prehistory, history, and archaeology as well as possibly revisit the site to get to know it better, we strongly recommend our much more in-depth guidebook to the city – *The Secrets of Ephesus*. It gives you not only a much wider perspective concerning Ephesus, but also provides a guided tour of the lovely nearby town called Selçuk with its numerous historical mosques but also impressive fortress with the Basilica of Saint John, the much neglected site of the ancient Temple of Artemis and small but comprehensive Ephesus Museum. Moreover, it tells the story of the so-called House of Virgin Mary located in the vicinity of Ephesus, in the lovely spot on the Hill of Nightingales.

The Secrets of Ephesus at Amazon.com

Other books from Turkish Archaeological News

Bibliography

Ancient sources

1. Aelian, Historical Miscellany
2. Appian, Civil Wars
3. Callimachus, Hymn to Artemis
4. Cassius Dio, History of Rome
5. Constantine the Rhodian, Description of the Church of the Holy Apostles in Constantinople
6. Eusebius, Church History
7. Gregory of Tours, Gloria Martyrum
8. Herodotus, Histories
9. Hesiod, Theogony
10. Homer, Iliad
11. Homer, Odyssey
12. Julius Caesar, Commentaries on the Civil War
13. Marcus Tullius Cicero, Letters to Atticus
14. Pausanias, Description of Greece
15. Philostratus, Lives of the Sophists
16. Pliny the Elder, Natural History
17. Pliny the Younger, Letters
18. Plutarch, Lives
19. Polybius, Histories
20. Polyaenus, Stratagems
21. Procopius of Caesarea, Secret History
22. Procopius of Caesarea, The Buildings
23. Strabo, The Geography
24. Tacitus, Annals

25. Theodosius the Pilgrim, De situ terrae sanctae
26. Thucydides, History of the Peloponnesian War
27. Titus Flavius Josephus, Against Apion
28. Titus Flavius Josephus, Antiquities of the Jews
29. Vitruvius, Ten Books on Architecture
30. Xenophon, Anabasis

Holy books

1. Bible, New International Version, https://www.biblica.com/bible/
2. Quran, https://quran.com/

Travellogues

1. F. V. J. Arundell, Discoveries in Asia Minor, Including a Description of the Ruins of Several Ancient Cities, Especially Antioch of Pisidia
2. E. Çelebi, Seyâhatnâme
3. R. Chandler, Travels in Asia Minor and Greece, 1825
4. C. Cockerell, Travels in southern Europe and the Levant, 1810-1817. The journal of C.R. Cockerell, 1903
5. Cyriacus of Ancona, Commentaria
6. L. Laborde, Voyage de l'Asie mineure, 1838
7. W. M. Leake, Journal of a tour in Asia Minor, with comparative remarks on the ancient and modern geography of that country
8. R. Muntaner, Chronicle, translated by Lady Goodenough, Cambridge, Ontario, 2000
9. R. Pococke, A description of the East, and some other countries, 1743
10. T. Smith, Remarks upon the manners, religion and government of the Turks, 1678
11. J. Spon, G. Wheler, Voyage d'Italie, de Dalmatie, de Grèce et du Levant, 1678
12. G. Wheler, A Journey Into Greece, 1682

Books and papers

1. T. Acar, Architecture of the Islamic Frontier: Architectural Sources and Urbanism in the Aydinid Principality (1304-1390), The University of Texas at Austin, 2018
2. I. Adenstedt, B. Thuswaldner, The Byzantine Palace of Ephesus: Reconstruction of the Tetraconch Hall, in: Proceedings of the 14th International Congress "Cultural Heritage and New Technologies", November 2009, Vienna, 2010
3. Z. Ákos, The context of medical competitions in Ephesus, in: Acta Antiqua Academiae Scientiarum Hungaricae, Volume 54, Issue 4, 2016
4. E. Akurgal, Ancient Civilizations and Ruins of Turkey, 11th ed., Net Turistik, Istanbul, 2011
5. A. Bammer, A Peripteros of the Geometric Period in the Artemision of Ephesus, in: Anatolian Studies, Volume 40, 1990
6. A. Bammer, L. Moens, U. Muss, The geological background of the architecture in the Artemision of Ephesus, in: Anatolia Antiqua, Tome 21, 2013
7. M. Beard, The skeleton of Cleopatra's sister? Steady on, in: A don's life, 2009
8. L. Bevilacqua, Recycling Myths in Byzantine Art: Spolia on the Gate of Persecution in Ephesus, in: Recycling Myths. Proceedings of the International Colloquium, Lisbon, 2012
9. J. M. Bloom, On the transmission of designs in early Islamic architecture, in: Muqarnas Online, 1992
10. J. Breder, H. Bumke, Die Kulte von Didyma im Licht neu entdeckter Bauten, in: Antike Welt, 2016/2
11. J. Bremmer, Priestly Personnel of the Ephesian Artemision: Anatolian, Persian, Greek and Roman Aspects, in: Practitioners of the Divine: Greek Priests and Religious Officials from Homer to Heliodorus, 2008
12. F. Brenk, Artemis of Ephesos: An Avant Garde Goddess, in: Kernos 11/1998
13. M. Carter, Archiereis and Asiarchs: A Gladiatorial Perspective,

in: Greek, Roman, and Byzantine Studies 44, 2004

14. M. Cottier, M. H. Crawford, et al. (editors), The Customs Law of Asia, Oxford, 2008
15. J. Dallaway, Constantinople, Ancient and Modern, with Excursions to the Shores and Islands of the Archipelago and to the Troad
16. R. G. Edmonds III, The Ephesia Grammata: Logos Orphaikos or Apolline Alexima pharmaka?, in: The Getty Hexameters: Poetry, Magic, and Mysteries in Ancient Selinous, ed. Christopher Faraone & Dirk Obbink, Oxford, 2013
17. S. P. Ellis, Theories of Circulation in Roman Houses, in: Theoretical Roman archaeology and architecture, Glasgow, 1999
18. A. C. Emmerich, The Dolorous Passion of Our Lord Jesus Christ, 2013
19. A. C. Emmerich, The Life of the Blessed Virgin Mary, Charlotte, 2004
20. K. Eren, Ionian sanctuaries and the mediterranean world in the seventh century BC, in: Proceedings of the 15th Symposium on Mediterrean Archaeology, held at the University of Catania 3-5 March 2011
21. E. Falkener, Ephesus and the Temple of Diana, 1862
22. S. Finley, Celsus Library of Ephesus: The Man and the City behind the Famous Façade, w: International Journal of Libraries and Information Studies, 2014
23. C. Foss, Ephesus After Antiquity: A Late Antique, Byzantine, and Turkish City, Cambridge University Press, Cambridge, 1979
24. C. Foss, Stephanus, Proconsul of Asia, and Related Statues, in: Harvard Ukrainian Studies, Vol. 7, Okeanos: Essays presented to Ihor Ševčenko on his Sixtieth Birthday by his Colleagues and Students, 1983
25. J. Freely, Children of Achilles. The Greeks in Asia Minor since the Days of Troy, I.B. Tauris, London, 2010
26. J. Freely, The Western Shores of Turkey, Tauris Parke Paperbacks, London, 2006

27. J. Harrison, The First Urban Churches 3: Ephesus, Atlanta, 2018
28. F. Hueber, Ephesos – Gebaute Geschichte, Mainz am Rhein, 1997
29. F. Hueber, Zur städtebaulichen Entwicklung des Hellenistisch-römischen Ephesos: Phylen, Embolos, Olympieion, Horologion, Staathalterpalast, Auditorium, Parthermonument, Marienkirche, in: Istanbuler Mitteilungen 47, 1997
30. K. E. Jessen, Portraits of Livia in context: an analysis of distribution through the application of geographic information systems, Iowa, 2013
31. A. H. M. Jones, The Greeks under the Roman Empire, Dumbarton Oaks Papers, 1963
32. C. P. Jones, The Olympieion and the Hadrianeion at Ephesos, in: The Journal of Hellenic Studies, 1993
33. F. Kanz and K. Grossschmidt, Dying in the arena: the osseous evidence from Ephesian gladiators, in: Roman Amphitheatres and Spectacula, a 21st-century Perspective: Papers from an International Conference Held at Chester, 16th-18th February, 2007
34. F. Kanz and K. Grossschmidt, Head injuries of Roman gladiators, in: Forensic Science International, 2006
35. N. Karydis, The evolution of the Church of St. John at Ephesos during the early Byzantine period, in: Jahreshefte des österreichischen archäologischen Institutes in Wien 84.84, 2016
36. M. Kerschner, Die Ionische Wanderung im Lichte neuer archäologischer Forschungen in Ephesos, in: Eckart Olshausen, Holger Sonnabend (ed.), Troianer sind wir gewesen – Migrationen in der antiken Welt. Stuttgarter Kolloquium zur Historischen Geographie des Altertums, 8, 2002, Stuttgart, 2006
37. D. Knibbe, Das Parther Monument von Ephesos: (Parthersieg)altar derArtemis (und Kenotaph des L. Verus) an der Triodos, in: Berichte und Materialien des Österreichischen

Archäologischen Instituts, 1991

38. A. Külzer, Reconstructing the Past in a changing Landscape. Reflections on the Area of Ephesus and other Sites in Western Asia Minor, in: Gephyra, nr 16, 2018
39. A. Külzer, Roads and Routes. Communication Networks in the Hinterland of Ephesos, in: Proceedings of the International Conference at the Research Center for Anatolian Civilizations, Koç University, Istanbul, 30th November – 2nd December 2012
40. A. Landskron, Architectural ornament under the Flavian dynasty in Asia Minor: The case of the altar of the Temple of Domitian in Ephesus, in: Thiasos Monografie X, 2016
41. S. Ladstätter, Ephesos from Late Antiquity until the Middle Ages. An Archaeological Introduction, in: Proceedings of the International Conference at the Research Center for Anatolian Civilizations, Koç University, Istanbul, 30th November – 2nd December 2012
42. S. Ladstätter, The So-called Imperial Cult Temple for Domitian in Ephesos, in: D. Schowalter, S. Ladstätter, St. Friesen,Ch. Thomas (Ed.), Religion in Ephesos Reconsidered. Archaeology of Spaces, Structures, and Objects. Supplements to Novum Testamentum 177, Leiden, 2019
43. M. Ledger et al., Intestinal parasites from public and private latrines and the harbour canal in Roman Period Ephesus, Turkey (1st c. BCE to 6th c. CE), in: Journal of Archaeological Science: Reports, Vol. 21, 2018
44. Mary R. Lefkowitz and Maureen b. Fant (ed.), Women's Life in Greece & Rome: A Source Book in Translation, 2016
45. K. Leloux, The Campaign Of Croesus Against Ephesus: Historical & Archaeological Considerations, in: Polemos: Journal of Interdisciplinary Research on War and Peace (21-2), 2018
46. R. Lesser, The Nature of Artemis Ephesia, The McGill Journal of Classical Studies, Volume IV: 43-54, 2005-2006
47. S. Lösch, et al., Stable isotope and trace element studies on gladiators and contemporary Romans from Ephesus (Turkey,

2nd and 3rd Ct. AD) – implications for differences in diet, in: PloS One 9.10, 2014
48. B. C. McGing, The Ephesian Customs Law and the Third Mithradatic War, in: Zeitschrift für Papyrologie und Epigraphik, Bd. 109, 1995
49. E. Mitsi, Wheler's, George. "Travel, Memory and Authorship: George Wheler's A Journey into Greece (1682)", in: Restoration vol. 30, 2006
50. C. Mooney, Hekate: Her Role and Character in Greek Literature from before the fifth century BC, 1971
51. F. Oğuz, Filiz, Selçuk, Karakolyanı Mescidi, 1978
52. K. Otto-Dorn, Die Isa Bey Moschee in Ephesus, in: Istanbuler Forschungen, 17, Berlin, 1950
53. U. Outschar, Zur Deutung des Hadrianstempels an der Kuretenstraße, in: H. Friesinger and F. Krinzinger, 100 Jahre österreichische Forschungen in Ephesos, 1999
54. G. Öney et al., Early Ottoman Art: The Legacy of the Emirates, Izmir, 2013
55. Ü. Öziş, A. Atalay, Y. Özdemir, Hydraulic capacity of ancient water conveyance systems to Ephesus, in: Water Supply, Vol.14, Issue 6, 2014
56. D. Parrish, Architectural function and decorative programs in the terrace houses in Ephesos, in: Topoi, volume 7/2, 1997
57. H. Plommer, St. John's Church, Ephesus, in: Anatolian Studies, Volume 12, 1962
58. L. Pollard, The Quest for Classical Greece: Early Modern Travel to the Greek World, London, 2015
59. E. Poulin, The Holy Virgin's House, The True Story of its Discovery, Istanbul, 1999
60. S. Price, Rituals and Power: The Roman Imperial Cult in Asia Minor, Cambridge, 1986
61. A. Pülz, S. Ladstätter, Meryemana bei Ephesos. Zur archäologischen Untersuchung des Jahres 2003, Vienna, 2006
62. U. Quatember, The "Temple of Hadrian" on Curetes Street in Ephesus: new research into its building history, in: Journal

of Roman Archaeology, 23, 2010

63. U. Quatember, B. Thuswaldner, R. Kalasek, B. Breuckmann, Ch. Bathow, The Virtual and Physical Reconstruction of the Octagon and Hadrian's Temple in Ephesus, in: Scientific Computing and Cultural Heritage. Contributions in Mathematical and Computational Sciences, vol 3., Berlin, Heidelberg, 2013
64. G. M. Rodgers, The Sacred Identity of Ephesos: foundation Myths of a Roman City, London, 1991
65. P. Scherrer, Ephesus: The new guide, 2000
66. M. Steskal, Bathing in Ephesos in the Byzantine and Turkish Period, in: Proceedings of the International Conference at the Research Center for Anatolian Civilizations, Koç University, Istanbul, 30th November – 2nd December 2012
67. M. Steskal, Wandering cemeteries, in: 2èmes Rencontres d'archéologie de l'IFEA: Le Mort dans la ville Pratiques, contextes et impacts des inhumations intra-muros en Anatolie, du début de l'Age du Bronze à l'époque romaine, Istanbul, 2011
68. F. Stock et al., In search of the harbours: New evidence of Late Roman and Byzantine harbours of Ephesus, in: Quaternary International, 2013
69. V. M. Strocka, The Celsus Library in Ephesus, in: Ancient libraries in Anatolia : libraries of Hattusha, Pergamon, Ephesus, Nysa, Ankara, 2003
70. L. E. Tanner, Some Representations of St. Edward the Confessor in Westminster Abbey and Elsewhere, in: Journal of the British Archaeological Association 15.1, 1952
71. H. Thür, Arsinoë IV, eine Schwester Kleopatras VII, Grabinhaberin des Oktogons von Ephesos? Ein Vorschlag, in: Jahreshefte des Österreichischen Archäologischen Instituts, vol. 60, 1990
72. P. Vădan, Ephesos after Alexander, Socio-Political Transformations in Western Asia Minor during the Early Hellenistic Period, Master Thesis, McGill University, Montreal, February, 2011

73. H. Wankel, Die Inschriften von Ephesos, Inschriften griechischer Städte aus Kleinasien 2, Bonn, 1979-1984
74. M. Wilson, Biblical Turkey, Istanbul, 2012
75. S. K. Yetkin, The Evolution of Architectural Form in Turkish Mosques (1300-1700), in: Studia Islamica No. 11, 1959
76. P. Yoncacı, Roman urban space framed by colonnades: Mediating between myth, memory and history in Ephesus, Master Thesis, Middle East Technical University, 2007
77. Ç. Yüksel, A Tale of Two Port Cities: Ayasuluk (Ephesus) and Balat (Miletus) during the Beyliks Period, in: Al-Masāq, Journal of the Medieval Mediterranean, 2019

Museum with Ephesus-related exhibits

1. Efes Arkeoloji Müzesi (Ephesus Archaeological Museum), Selçuk, Turkey
2. Arkeoloji ve Entografya Müzesi (Archaeological and Ethnographical Museum), Izmir, Turkey
3. Izmir Tarih ve Sanat Müzesi (Izmir Museum of History and Art), Izmir, Turkey
4. Ephesos-Museum der Antikensammlung des Kunsthistorischen Museums Wien (Ephesos Museum), Vienna, Austria
5. The British Museum, London, England
6. Ashmolean Museum, Oxford, England
7. Woburn Art Gallery, Milton Keynes, England
8. Musei Capitolini (Capitoline Museums), Rome, Italy

About the Author

Izabela Miszczak is the editor of TurkishArchaeoNews.net website devoted to the cultural heritage of Asia Minor. She holds a master diploma in social sciences with the specialization in the sociology of culture. She has authored several publications in the area of political studies and social sciences. She has written many guidebooks in Polish and English. She is also the editor of TurcjaWSandalach.pl portal for independent travellers. She lives in Poland with her husband, two kids, and a dog called Madzia.

About Turkish Archaeological News

TAN stands for Turkish Archaeological News, https://TurkishArchaeoNews.net/, was created in 2013 to provide news about the latest archaeological discoveries in Turkey and neighbouring regions.

The project has been developed into a travel portal, dedicated to history buffs who visit Turkey searching for historical buildings, ancient ruins, and fascinating museums. TAN website publishes texts about such places as well as the news concerning archaeological excavations and discoveries. All our texts are illustrated with original photos that TAN editorial team has taken during our travels around Turkey. We have been visiting this beautiful country regularly since 2004, and the website, as well as TAN Travel Guides, are the reflection of our ongoing fascination with Asia Minor.

Printed in Great Britain
by Amazon

58470628R00066